Where does intersection happen? Is it a peaceful encounter or a violent collision? Can these art objects coexist, or are they so disparate that they must reside in parallel universes? What is modernism? How can art transcend traditional categories and make connections with works of other styles and genres?

MODERNIST INTERSECTIONS

Modernist Intersections: The Tia Collection

May 14 - October 9, 2016

THE UNIVERSITY OF ARIZONA
MUSEUM OF ART

Foreword

Collecting is part art and part craft. Collectors seek, locate, acquire, organize, catalogue, store, and preserve things. Over time, collectors develop finely honed skills that make them adept at their craft, but the art of collecting is in sharing a collection with others, displaying it, discovering connections, and inspiring dialogue. The secret to the art of collecting is the passion and purpose behind the desire to collect.

Collectors, like curators, can be generalists or specialists; some start off as one and evolve over time as their tastes change. Most have criteria for inclusion, whether broad or specific, and the criteria matures over time. For some, collecting is a lifelong pursuit; others discover collecting as adults. Beginning collectors range from novices to experts in their area of interest, but as collections grow the collector's eye becomes sharper.

Collections bring great joy to those who create them, but the public often does not get to delight in viewing these treasures. In rare instances, private collections are created with the intention that they be shared with the public for the greater good. This is one of those instances.

The Tia Collection is being created with the purest motive: to share the collector's zeal for art with a broad audience. Gathered over the course of a mere nine years, the collection is a vast mélange of artistic styles and genres. The collector, who prefers anonymity, is building the collection in honor of his teenage daughter, Tia. Forsaking the limelight, the collector prefers to let the artwork—and the artists—sparkle.

Selfless acts of philanthropy such as The Tia Collection are what make the art world so extraordinary. I became acquainted with the collection in 2010 and the collector in 2013, whilst organizing the first-ever exhibition of works solely from The Tia Collection. The collector is modest yet sophisticated, cultured yet unassuming, successful yet soft-spoken, and most of all charitable. Discovering a love of art as an adult was such a joy that he determined to share that delight with his family—particularly his young daughter Tia—and the public.

I have enjoyed working with Laura Finlay Smith, The Tia Collection curator, who works in tandem with the collector to continually add new works of art to the collection. I was thrilled to discover the breadth of The Tia Collection after joining The University of Arizona Museum of Art (UAMA), having previously only been familiar with the Western American artwork in the collection. I learned about the extensive 20th and 21st century modernist works in collection just recently.

The concept for this exhibition developed shortly after I arrived at the UAMA as Director in 2014. Initially, Laura approached me with the idea of collaborating. When she learned of the UAMA's renowned modernism collection, and I learned of The Tia Collection's complementary holdings, the synergy became apparent. We approached UAMA Curator of Exhibitions and Education, Olivia Miller, with the idea; it was she who conceived the approach of pairing or grouping works from the collection based on intersections between the artworks. This approach offers the opportunity to view the collection, which spans three continents, through a variety of lenses.

The exhibition planning process was collaborative and flexible. Laura and I viewed the works in person in Santa Fe, New Mexico to make an initial wish list, which was honed by Olivia, who then faced the daunting task of creating the groupings and drawing the connections. In the interest of pulling the curtain back on the curatorial process a bit, it's worth noting that the artworks could have been organized in any number of different ways. A piece might appear on the surface to be about the environment, but upon further examination might be about composition or motion, even rhythm. As a team, we discussed whether works should be grouped in pairs or threes or fours; in the end we opted for all of the above, allowing for a much more dynamic exhibition.

At first glance, it is not necessarily obvious why each of the works in the exhibition is considered modernist. The definitions of modernist (and all of the "isms" that fall under it) are myriad; we embraced the broadest interpretation of the term, allowing us to re-examine these works in a new context. The process was fluid, and works were included for many reasons.

Modernists break down the conventional formulas of representation, adopt new techniques, examine subjects from a multitude of viewpoints, and, generally speaking, eschew realism.

Alice Neel *The Black Boys*

They draw attention to the artistic process and the materials used in creating a work of art. Experimentation, aesthetic introspection, and a re-examination of existence are all hallmarks of modernism. One or more elements of these traits can be found in each of the works in *Modernist Intersections*.

Many of these works defy expectations in order to pressure viewers into questioning their own assumptions about the subject— or about art in general. Some of the artists use unconventional processes, pushing against traditional boundaries. While a few of the works border on realism, others span the spectrum from Expressionism to Abstract Expressionism to Minimalism. The latter works capture the essence of the identity of the subject by eliminating all nonessential concepts, forms, or features, creating the maximum effect with a minimum of elements.

One thing is certain, the artwork in *Modernist Intersections* is sure to evoke emotions and kindle dialogue. The intersections— atmosphere, cycles, disruption, redemption, environment, distortion, juxtaposition, transcendence, and departure, to name a few—suggest the rich narrative embedded in these works.

In the pages that follow, you'll read about the stories associated with the works in *Modernist Intersections*; these stories are what make the artwork come alive. We chose multiple authors for their varying expertise, as the artwork spans more than one hundred years and includes painting, sculpture, photography, and mixed-media. The authors' voices vary, much like the works in the exhibition and the definitions of modernist. Readers will see the artwork from multiple viewpoints, making the tales behind the art more intriguing.

As you read, I invite you to consider interpretation, suggestion, perception, and reaction.

– W. James Burns, Ph.D.
Director, The University of Arizona Museum of Art
Acting Administrative Director, Center for Creative Photography

Allan Houser *Thinking of Him*

Modernist Intersections

John Baldessari's *Intersection* series includes photographs with many images arranged in provocative ways. Some works are composed of two overlapping images, while others, such as *Intersection Series: Landscape and Caravan (with Tall Tree)* (2002) (right), connect images together. Although each work in the series is unique, they all share the same basic format—uniting disparate images in a way that juxtapose or overlap. The absurdity of the combinations is part of the joy of looking at the work. Scenes such as a seascape and a keyboardist come together in order to subvert the traditional understanding of certain ideas and to create new meaning. Using *Intersection Series: Landscape and Caravan (with Tall Tree)* as a starting point, *Modernist Intersections: The Tia Collection* expands on this idea of bringing artworks together in new ways.

Although not religious in the traditional sense of the word, museums are sacred spaces, functioning as the keepers of cultural memory and uniting relics of human creativity that were created worlds apart.[i] The museum's responsibility is enormous—to preserve these objects in perpetuity and make them accessible to the everyday person. Apart from the obvious professional display, the experience of seeing art in a museum is different than in a home or another setting. At the museum, the art is displayed within an educational context, which is often determined by curatorial choices, educational resources, and availability of other art objects.

Museum exhibitions allow viewers the opportunity to experience the work of art among other objects and to make connections. A curatorial voice provides visitors with guidance for their viewing experience, but ultimately viewers form their own opinions and conclusions—it is "the visitors who enact the ritual."[ii] The purpose of this exhibition is twofold: first, to incite dialogue through the juxtaposition of artworks and, second, to demonstrate the malleability of the boundaries of modernism. The works in *Modernist Intersections* have been clustered and arranged in order to inspire questions and encourage active looking. Viewers are invited to activate the dialogue between the artworks to elicit connections and meaning. Although value judgments certainly often arise out of comparative analysis, it is not the intention of the exhibition to pit one artist against the other. Instead, it is to find commonalities between artworks, some of which were created decades and miles apart.

Some connections are created through the formal elements of the art object. For example, Tyeb Mehta's *Portrait of Husain* (1975) seems quite different from William Eggleston's *Untitled* (1970). Yet upon closer inspection, it is clear that the use of color is fundamental for each artist in setting the mood of the image. Other times it is subject matter and artistic intention that provide the link, as is the case with Henry Moore's *Madonna and Child* (1943) and Francis Newton Souza's *The Virgin of Northampton* (1957). The beauty of an exhibition such as this is that seemingly diverse works can be fused, co-existing and communicating in the same world. Although the arrangements have been pre-selected for the viewer, it is when the visitor enters the conversation that the meaning really evolves.

What viewers will also note is the fluidity of modern art and how its influence extends into contemporary and Western art. What exactly does it mean for a work of art to be described as modern? There is a temporal quality to the word, implying that it is something created in the not-too-distant past, but when one thinks of it in relation to the art historical movement of modernism, this is where the conversation really begins to get sticky. While a full description of the modernist movement is beyond the scope of this essay, suffice it to say that the birth of modernism reacted to the Industrial Revolution and various societal changes that occurred in the 19th and 20th centuries, allowing for new experimentation in art. Color, materials, and subject matter were manipulated in new ways in order to eschew the traditional thought that art needed to be realistic and filled with moral relevance. This exhibit includes contemporary works that are decades removed from the modernist movement, but their existence would not have been possible without the groundwork that was laid by modern artists. Artworks that are also commonly classified as Western can also be seen as having modern tendencies.

As this exhibit shows, there is something modern to be found in each of these works. For example, Nicolai Fechin's *Winter Landscape, Taos* (c. 1927) presents a beautiful view of a snowy landscape. While clearly it is an example of Western painting, the chunky brushstrokes also show influence from Cézanne, one of the most instrumental

©John Baldessari. Courtesy Marian Goodman and Spruth Magers

John Baldessari *Intersection Series: Landscape and Caravan (with Tall Tree)*

figures in the modernist movement. Christopher Wool's *Untitled* (1988) poses similar questions that many works of modern art do, challenging the idea of medium, repetition, and subject matter. At once it pulls elements from Pop Art, Minimalism, and Abstract Expressionism, in order to create a new kind of art.

Art historians have been self-aware for quite some time regarding the constrictive nature of the traditional structure of their discipline.[iii] Most art history textbooks still favor a chronological approach and place seminal artworks into neat categories. As Kurt Forster explains, "The daily work of art historians appears to be founded on three basic concepts: history of style, artistic biography, and the tradition of imagery (or iconography). All three are constructs that provide a scaffolding around which a diverse and incoherent mass of information can be organized, but they have the disadvantage of being basically static in nature."[iv] This is not to say that art historical categories are not necessary. They absolutely are. One can talk about the style of a work of art all day, but to suggest it has nothing to do with the context in which it was created is naïve at best. Jackson Pollock would never have created his drip paintings during the Renaissance—there simply were neither the resources nor the long development of abstract art to support such an idea. It would never have entered a Renaissance artist's consciousness to paint the way Pollock did.

While the recognition of historical context is essential to understanding human culture, it is not the sole way to approach these objects. This exhibit does not displace art history's role, it merely shifts it and allows the categorical walls to collapse for the sake of comparison. Put simply, it allows the works to intersect. These connections illuminate features about a work of art that otherwise might not be as noticeable. They also allow the meaning and function of the work to transcend the object itself, encouraging viewers to think critically about what they see. As Robert Nelson suggests, art history "can be unmade or re-sited, re-structured, and re(-)formed, and what has become tangible and reified can revert to mere heuristic category." Above all, it demonstrates that art is boundless. While traditional art historical categories have profound importance, breaking out of those boundaries can be freeing. John Baldessari said it best: "I think art, if it's meaningful at all, is a conversation with other artists. You say something, they say something, you move back and forth."[vi]

– Olivia Miller
Curator of Exhibitions and Education,
The University of Arizona Museum of Art

i Carol Duncan, *Civilizing Rituals: Inside Public Art Museums* (London: Routledge, 1995), p. 8.

ii Ibid, p. 12.

iii Just a few relevant examples include, Donald Brook, "Art History?" *History and Theory* 43 (February, 2004):1-17; Robert S. Nelson, "The Map of Art History," The Art Bulletin 79 (1997): p. 28-40; and Donald Preziosi, *Rethinking Art History: Meditations on a Coy Science* (New Haven: Yale University Press, 1989).

iv Kurt W. Forster, "Critical History of Art, or Transfiguration of Values?" *New Literary History* Vol. 3, No. 3 (Spring, 1972) p. 459.

v Robert S. Nelson, "The Map of Art History," *The Art Bulletin* 79 (1997): p. 28.

vi Interview by David Salle, October 9, 2013
http://www.interviewmagazine.com/art/john-baldessari/

The Tia Collection
Diverse Cultures, Histories, and Aesthetics
A Note from the Collector

There is an enduring tradition of artists from all over the world exploring and sometimes even settling far from their homeland. This tradition can be placed in the broader historical arc of the migration of peoples over centuries, a movement that has resulted in a rich intermingling of cultures.

If migration, because of its magnitude and often involuntary nature, creates rapid and permanent change, travel — through integration, adaptation and understanding — ignites a cultural evolution that is slower, more subtle perhaps, but enduring all the same. Through travel we witness and experience the changing social web of a country.

My own travels from a distant country to Europe and the United States led to the creation of this collection, surprising many on both ends of the world. Different locales have offered me a treasure trove of experiences, and a visit to New Mexico years ago sparked a fascination for Southwestern historical, contemporary, and Native American art. I slowly added these artworks to my existing collection, which featured inspiring pieces from my own country and across Europe.

Travel is a life-changing pursuit, and mind-expanding experiences like these shape who we are. Yet, it's not enough to passively comprehend our experiences intellectually. We must act on our understanding, and be driven by it, so that we can contribute value to an ever-changing world.

Collectors tend to collect, most of the time, for the sheer love of it. The overriding impulse has its origins in pure positivity, in sharing the joy we get from fine art. But there's also another, equally important part of our mission as collectors: to encourage artists to create what is hidden deep within them and not just what the market blesses. The artists I have encountered and admired, indeed envied, have kept nothing of themselves from their work, conveying to viewers their sweeping messages of emotion, philosophy, beauty. Many artists are driven to continue the traditions of the Old Masters while also bringing forward unique ideas. Sometimes they have concealed thoughts and depths that can only be expressed through their chosen medium. Whatever the impetus behind their work, they must be encouraged. Their gifts must be acknowledged and supported. Their work must be shown, to those who share their culture and to those who do not. Let history be the only judge of them.

At its heart, The Tia Collection is a global collection. It is a reflection of my travels and of my deep admiration for art of all genres and geographical origins. It is not a collection only for my appreciation—that would be far too confining. These are works that must be displayed for the world to see, admire, acknowledge, celebrate. They are a testimony to the value of diverse cultures, histories, and aesthetics.

March, 2016

Alexander Calder *La Botte* (maquette)

Erin Currier *The Raft*

MOTION MOOD

DISTORTION

LANDSCAPE

ENVIRONMENT EQUINE

TEXT

ARCHETYPES

REDEMPTION

MADONNA & CHILD

COMPOSITION

DISRUPTION

ATMOSPHERE

JUXTAPOSITION

CYCLES

EVOKE

TRANSCENDENCE

MEDIUM

ASSEMBLAGE

RHYTHM

WALLS

ABSTRACTION

DEPARTURE

Each of these paintings uses Pop Art aesthetics to explore iconic symbols—
in one case that of the cowboy and in the other the Queen of England. How do
these two figures relate to the idea of celebrity? How do they reflect popular
culture and shape views of the United States and the United Kingdom?

ARCHETYPES

Bill Schenck *Gathering Mustangs*

Andy Warhol *Queen Elizabeth II of the United Kingdom*

Bill Schenck

Schenck uses a combination of Pop Art and photorealism in his contemporary renderings of the American West. He paints in a flat, reductive style; colors are hard-edged and do not blend with one another. As with many of his works, *Gathering Mustangs* reflects the artist's fondness for bold colors and strong compositions.

Born and educated in the Midwest, Schenck found success in the art world of 1970s New York, reverentially appropriating other artists' work to create striking pieces full of commentary about the American West, where he made his home since the late 1970s.

Gathering Mustangs is a perfect example of Schenck's appropriation. The basis for this painting can be found in a Nicholas Eggenhofer black-and-white drawing from a pulp fiction Western magazine. Schenck projected the original drawing and added the mesas in the background, infusing the painting with his signature palette.

First used in the mid-1980s, this image has reappeared in Schenck's work for the past thirty years. *Gathering Mustangs* is paired with a Warhol screenprint in this exhibition. Both works contain Pop Art elements. Schenck muses: "The pairing is fitting. Warhol was another appropriator of images."

When asked how this work is modernist, Schenck replied: "It's obviously modernist, because it's a paint-by-number system. That system emerged as a commercial endeavor in the late 1940s/early 1950s. I took same approach as those artists but extended it to an extreme degree."

Lest his work be considered realism, Schenck further explains, "My paintings and photographs represent less and less what is out there in the 'real world.' Even the painted landscapes are becoming more invented. The process is a reorganization of 'real world' objects, figures, and space into an interior dialogue that are representations of how I interpret my connection to these objects."

– James Burns

Andy Warhol

This is one of four variations on *Queen Elizabeth II of the United Kingdom* that Andy Warhol made for his *Reigning Queens* series. The series also features Margrethe II of Denmark, Beatrix of the Netherlands, and Ntombi of Swaziland. Far from being a random selection of royal women, these four were chosen by Warhol because they each occupied their respective thrones not as the wife of a king but as queen regnant.

Warhol often used existing photographs taken by himself or others as a starting point for his portraits. In this case, he converted Peter Grungeon's 1977 official portrait of Queen Elizabeth II's Silver Jubilee into an iconic symbol of royalty. The addition of brilliant color, contour lines, and shapes flattens and artificializes the image. As with his other portraits, such as those of Marilyn Monroe, *Queen Elizabeth II of the United Kingdom* encourages the viewer to question the cultural ideal of celebrity.

– Olivia Miller

These two works depict the New Mexican landscape in wildly divergent ways. How do artists manipulate medium in order to create mood?

ATMOSPHERE

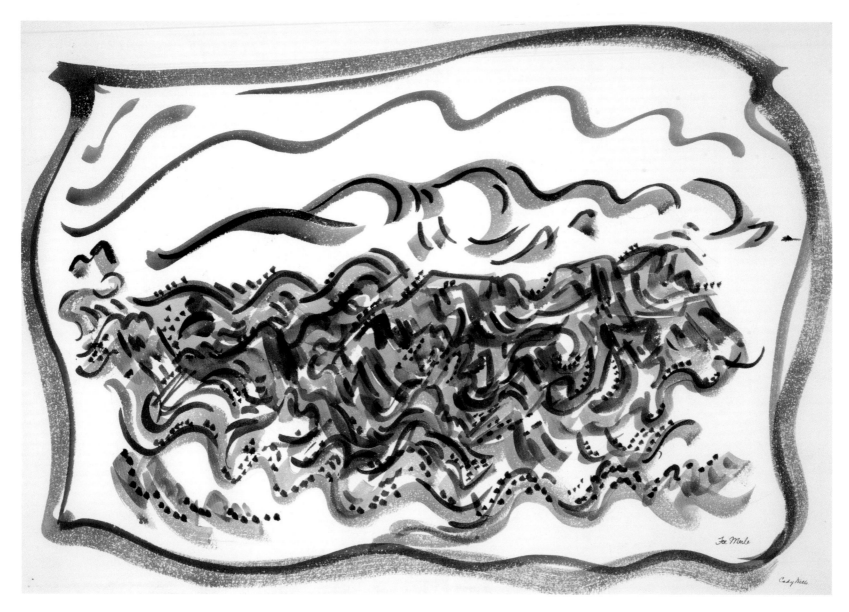

Cady Wells *New Mexico Landscape*

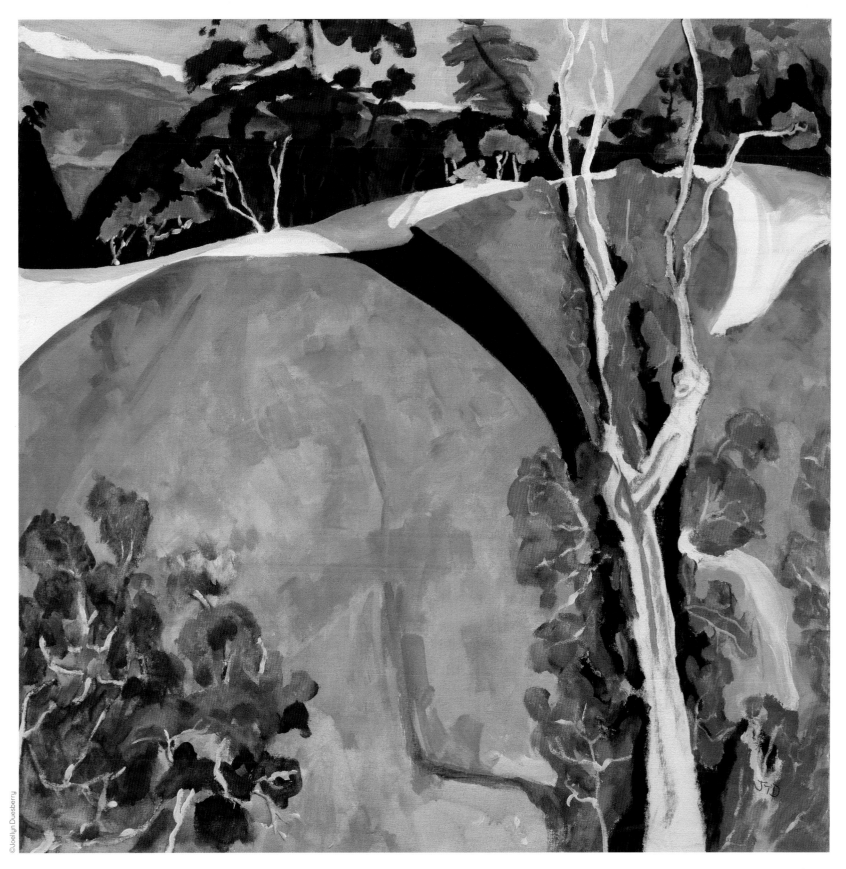

Joellyn Duesberry *New Mexico, Red Earth*

Cady Wells

As Cady Wells stated, "My approach to painting is rooted in my feelings for and about the forms and objects in nature and in life that are beautiful, exciting and stimulating to me as a human being; and in my desire to evoke similar sensations in others... [The] creative process in painting—the act itself—is based on my needs and wishes to share with others what I cannot share in any other form." As he began developing his visual vocabulary during his early years in New Mexico, this premise became the basis for his work, with exciting results.

New Mexico Landscape shows how Wells worked the entire sheet of paper, leaving some areas completely blank, completing the composition in a fresh unencumbered manner. The brush strokes are fluid, lyrical, and almost calligraphic in nature. Black is set against a vivid blue and used to emphasize the undulating hills and craggy arroyos. The influence of Wells' teacher, Andrew Dasburg, can be seen in the works from the early 1930s. His style set him apart from his Santa Fe and Taos modernist contemporaries.

– Laura Finlay Smith

Joellyn Duesberry

New Mexico, Red Earth is one of self-taught landscape painter Joellyn Duesberry's favorite works from her long and distinguished
career. She has painted the landscapes of New Mexico and Colorado
for decades, establishing her reputation as a regionalist with a clear
focus. This reputation overlooks the works she has created around the
world and discounts Duesberry's self-identification as a modernist.

A 1986 National Endowment for the Arts painting grant afforded
Duesberry the opportunity to study under famed California modernist
Richard Diebenkorn for a month, changing the trajectory of her career
as an artist. The time she spent with Diebenkorn prompted her to move
from Manhattan to Colorado, where she began to explore the geometry
of the Western landscape.

In 1989, she painted a winter stream bed at Ghost Ranch, near
Abiquiú, New Mexico. That painting is the nucleus of a body of work
spanning twenty-five years, including *New Mexico, Red Earth*. In
July 2012, Duesberry began to isolate the elements of this theme
that she found most fascinating. She recalls: "I cropped until I had the
absolute essence of the design. That's what the modernist is. I cropped
until I had an old memory and brought it into the present through my
imagination. This is not an outdoor observation. It is straight from my
memory, using a tiny postcard."

Duesberry considers *New Mexico, Red Earth* to be the "final
iteration of a lifetime obsession with a scene. At Ghost Ranch there is
a creek that freezes; it has steep banks with cypress trees. I left out the
roots. Some of the cypress trees are dying, but they are beautiful even
in death. I have always painted motifs of survival."

For this final iteration, Duesberry used acrylic rather than oil,
her traditional medium. The artist loves the colors and the details of
Western winters, and she remembers "the long and joyful process to
discovering the image at the heart of what I wanted to say. This is a
celebration of a fine old image, central to my theme of a screen of trees
and then a far view. It's a reduction, an irreducible element."

– James Burns

Using intersection and overlap, Baldessari and Friedlander combine photographic images in a humorous way. Do distortion and juxtaposition of objects make it easier or harder for viewers to uncover a narrative?

JUXTAPOSITION

Lee Friedlander *New York City*

John Baldessari *Intersection Series: Landscape and Caravan (with Tall Tree)*

Lee Friedlander

Nearing the age of eighty, Friedlander remains an unrelenting photographer with a prodigious output spanning more than half a century.

This image is from a body of work focused on shop windows and reflections, shot between 2003 and 2011 with a 35mm camera that he used at the beginning of his career. It shares the same title as its book cover—*Mannequin*, published by Fraenkel Gallery, in 2012.

The piece is emblematic of Friedlander's inimitable style, with its unsettling, sometimes puzzling reflections reminiscent of his earlier work that incorporated mirrors, glass walls, shop fronts, car windshields, and television sets.

This picture is almost surreal: a headless mannequin in a fitted dress with designer accessories and shapely legs. In place of the head and torso, we see instead clouds in the sky and the ubiquitous façade of a New York skyscraper. On her right stands another mannequin, one we almost miss, her sleeved arm almost touching her partner's and enveloping a sliver of the sky.

The camera is pointed upwards, so we do not see a reflection of the photographer. In employing this low-angle shot, Friedlander was probably aiming to make the model appear larger than life to emphasize her role as a fashion icon and as a symbol of consumerism.

While the storefront mannequin is often a staple subject of street photography, in the hands of a technical and artistic master like Friedlander, the image transcends cliché and becomes unmistakably his own.

– Ketaki Sheth

John Baldessari

In 2002, John Baldessari presented a new series of work, *Intersections*, which are reminiscent of the Stations of the Cross. Each piece is composed of two images—one vertical, the other horizontal—that meet, generating a third image where they overlap.

Intersection Series: Landscape and Caravan (with Tall Tree) has one image that comes from the cinema, with grainy black-and-white reflections; the other is a color photograph of the earth from afar, with the land vividly captured in high definition. The form that results in the intersection of the two resembles a tree. In the piece, photography, film, and painting interact with each other to create a visual diary of sorts, communicating a journey of crossed paths.

Baldessari sees art as a language wherein a word can be interpreted as an image, and vice versa. A teacher as well an an artist, he believes that his time in the classroom is equivalent, in many ways, to the act of making art. Teaching and art—both means of communication—cross-pollinate and affect each other.

In a 2013 interview with Susan Sollins, the artist said, "I got a real sense of moral obligation, and I think that's why I was a late starter in art, because art didn't seem to do anybody any good that I could see. It didn't heal bones; it didn't help people find shelter. Teaching juvenile delinquents was a real eye-opener for me, because they had a stronger need for art than I did. And they were criminals. We had no other shared values, but they cared more about art than I did. It dawned on me that it must provide some sort of spiritual nourishment—as terrible as that sounds—but it must."

– Sarah J. McDonald

This grouping prompts us to consider the many essential roles horses play in human lives, from religion to rural life to racing. The Cannon and Black paintings present calm and soothing equine images, while Davey and Singleton show us the power and speed of these animals. How are horses portrayed as symbols, and what is it they represent?

EQUINE

Randall Davey *Untitled (Horse & Rider)*

T.C. Cannon *All the Tired Horses in the Sun*

LaVerne Nelson Black *The Gathering*

Gib Singleton *Four Horsemen of the Apocalypse*

Randall Davey

The equestrian figure is one of the oldest traditions in portraiture, extending at least as far back as ancient Rome. Randall Davey, however, has taken this ancient ideal to a different level. This sculpture is not a static depiction of an emperor or solider on horseback, but rather portrays a jockey at the height of a race.

Although this sculpture is rendered in bronze, it is full of motion, an effect achieved through pose and texture. Davey enhances the illusion of movement by breaking the visual barrier of the sculpture's base; the horse's leg projects outward, as if about to gallop into the viewer's space.

Originally from New Jersey and educated at Robert Henri's School of Painting and at the Art Students League in New York, Davey moved to Santa Fe, where he became a member of the Santa Fe Art Colony and taught at the University of New Mexico in Albuquerque. In addition to the female nude and the still life, the horse was a common subject in Davey's art.

– Olivia Miller

T.C. Cannon

Often referred to as the van Gogh of Native American art, T.C. Cannon created work characterized by the use of bold colors and expressive organic shapes. Cannon was originally from Oklahoma but moved to Santa Fe in order to study at the Institute of American Indian Arts. Although traditional Native American themes surface in his work, his style also demonstrates modern sensibilities.

All the Tired Horses in the Sun depicts two horses grazing in an expansive field. While the horses are clearly the subject of the piece, Cannon makes the sky just as important—the low horizon line allows the bulk of the canvas to become taken over by the sunrise orange sky dotted with clouds.

Cannon was not interested in realism, but that was not the point of his work. Instead, he focused on the essence of the horses and the calming yet blissful mood of the outdoor landscape. The coloristic effects help to shape the mood of his paintings, as well as draw the viewer's eye to the horses.

– Olivia Miller

LaVerne Nelson Black

Originally from Wisconsin, LaVerne Nelson Black studied at the Chicago Academy of Fine Arts and did commercial art for newspapers before moving to New Mexico. Although he only lived in Taos for a couple of years, the region had a huge impact on the subject matter of his work, which was filled with scenes of horses and Native Americans set against mountainous backdrops.

This image shows a candid scene of a Native American gathering. Some figures are mounted on horseback, as if they have just arrived, while others gather around conversing. Although the scene is filled with people, Black has placed special emphasis on the horses. A white horse standing in profile is in the exact center of the canvas. A brown horse situated in the right foreground stares out at the viewer.

Black has captured the essence of the horses and demonstrated his technical abilities by presenting a horse from a profile view as well as a foreshortened frontal perspective. One can see that the horses, rather than being depicted as props, are rendered as essential to Native American daily life.

This painting (like others by Black) is naturally seen as a classic Western painting. However, the artist's painterly brushstrokes clearly reference the modernist penchant for texture and the celebration of paint on the surface of a canvas.

– Olivia Miller

Gib Singleton

Gib Singleton referred to himself as an "emotional realist," and his work expresses intense feelings through the use of texture, movement, and exaggerated proportions. Citing Frederic Remington as a key influence, Singleton moved from the Northeast to Santa Fe in order to produce Western art. Although he certainly explored many Western themes in his art, Biblical subject matter was just as important to his oeuvre.

During the last years of his life, themes of death, sacrifice, and redemption became a central part of his artistic production, and this sculpture is an example from that time period. Here Singleton has interpreted the Four Horsemen of the Apocalypse to reflect their specific characterizations in the Book of Revelation (6:1-8). He incorporated a colored patina for each horse, as well as the items in the riders' hands, to correspond with the written description.

In this work, one can see the intense power and speed of the horses, as their hooves topple off the edge of the sculpture and break out into the viewer's space. The faces of the men are striking as well—they have been greatly exaggerated, with dark sunken eyes that provoke fear in the viewer.

– Olivia Miller

These landscapes represent seasonal moods of New Mexico. How do texture, color, and point of view contribute to the tactile nature of the landscapes, allowing the viewer to experience the season?

CYCLES

Willard Nash *Springtime, Santa Fe*

Nicolai Fechin *Winter Landscape, Taos*

Willard Nash

Willard Nash was one of the earliest members of the Santa Fe Art Colony and a founding member of the young artists' group known as Los Cinco Pintores (or "The Five Painters"). Composed of Willard Nash, Jozef Bakos, Will Shuster, Fremont Ellis, and Walter Mruk, the group believed in experimenting freely with modernist painting methods. By 1921, Nash was regarded as one of the group's more sophisticated artists.

Andrew Dasburg—who was a part of New York's avant-garde artist society as well as a Taos modernist painter—became Nash's painting companion and teacher. He urged Nash to explore the structural principals of fragmented form made famous by Paul Cézanne, including the use of contour line as a means of dynamic expression. Form and color in painting took precedence over depiction of an object, and Nash's work became increasingly infused with an abstract simplicity and Cubist spirit.

In *Springtime, Santa Fe*, Nash captured the New Mexico landscape awakening from a long winter's sleep. Brilliant light plays across the hills, which are just beginning to turn green, while blooming fruit trees and deep blues in the sky set the mood for the day. Nash has approached this easily recognizable subject matter with a progressive and modern style of painting. The snow melting on the mountain peaks, a road leading from one side of the composition to the other, and adobe structures scattered throughout create a confluence of shapes and colors that result in an aesthetically satisfying work—a concept that was an utmost goal for the artist.

– Laura Finlay Smith

Nicolai Fechin

Winter Landscape, Taos is a beautiful example of Nicolai Fechin's work and indicative of the artist's style during his Taos period, combining a predilection for modern art while simultaneously capturing the realism of an intimate glimpse into the region's daily life.

Fechin wrote: "The artist must not forget that he is dealing with the entire canvas, and not with only one section of it. Regardless of what he sets out to paint, the problem in his work remains one and the same: with originality, to fill in his canvas and make of it an organic whole ... Technique should be considered only as a means to an end, but never the end in itself." (Mary Balcomb, *Nicolai Fechin*, San Cristobal, New Mexico, 1975)

Trained at the Imperial Academy in Leningrad, Fechin developed a quick and dramatic approach to painting. After immigrating to the United States in 1923 with his wife and young daughter, he immersed himself in the artistic community of New York. Discontented with city living, however, Fechin ventured west to California in 1926, traveling through the unique Southwest landscape of desert and mountains. When Fechin accepted an invitation from his friend and fellow portrait painter John Young-Hunter to stop in Taos, New Mexico, he became immediately enchanted with the history, landscape, and people of Taos Pueblo.

Fechin flourished in the bright light and intense, contrasting hues of the region. Using pure color applied directly to the canvas with broad strokes of a palette knife, he worked quickly to capture a sincere and direct form of the scene in front of him.

— Laura Finlay Smith

Balance is one of the hallmarks of a pleasing composition. Often artists disrupt balance in order to create meaning in an artwork. What are some of the implications of balance, both visual and otherwise? What does it mean when we disrupt that balance?

DISRUPTION

Alexander Calder *La Botte* (maquette)

Robert Mapplethorpe *Phillip Prioleau, 1979*

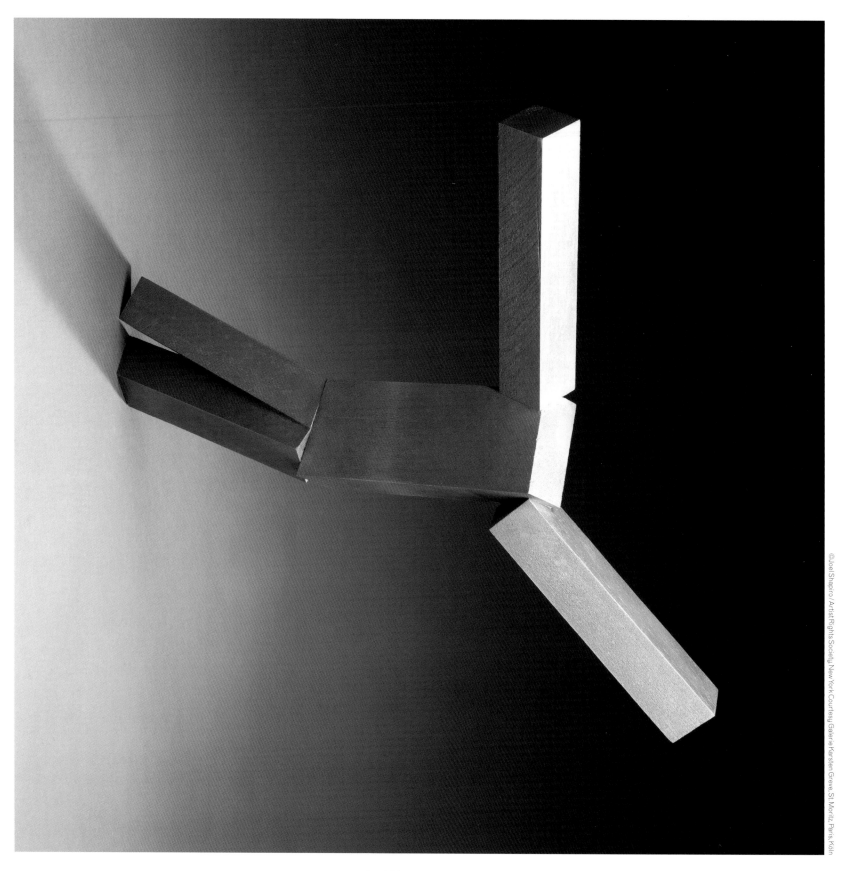

Joel Shapiro *Untitled*

Alexander Calder

The conceptual foundation for *La Botte* (The Boot) was begun in an earlier body of Calder's work, containing pieces that experimented with circus animals, circus performers, and models made from twisted wire, created while he was living in Paris, France.

Surrounded by his avant-garde artist friends, Calder's nature was social, never solitary. He had a penchant for the mechanical and the traditional, which made him a natural constructor. Those tendencies, combined with the art of play, both lyrical and poetic, created a movement that encompassed the artist and his public.

Calder employed his life's passion to entertain his guests, who in turn engaged themselves with the work. Just as his guests became stand-ins for the public at large, his scale models eventually became monuments, giant metal structures that stood out bravely in both urban and rural settings.

La Botte (maquette) contains multiple silhouette-like shapes that invite the viewer to explore the composition from all angles. Walking around the stabile, one might feel oneself to be in orbit around a sort of lightness of being. With his unique pioneering approach of researching the form, surface, and spirit of his silhouettes, Calder managed to modernize the art of sculpture.

Alexander Calder's work is eternally young. It plays, it experiments, and it breathes into its art life and strength. Fernand Léger wrote of the artist that "always with a smile, he pushed on the magic button and everything slowly turned, graciously ... the mobile sculpture was invented."

– Sarah J. McDonald

Robert Mapplethorpe

In *Phillip Prioleau*, the named body is placed on a pedestal, signaling that this work is more about surface and form than a literal representation of the figure. Overall, the image alludes to the type of classical beauty reflected in Renaissance sculptures, where there is taste for detail and a desire for perfection.

The photographic setting is staged in such a way that the piece becomes a pure understanding of form and light that reflects the sensual qualities of the human body. The position of the figure's head, hands, and feet bring to mind a crucified Christ—and, indeed, Mapplethorpe has said he wanted his pictures to be viewed as if they were altars.

It has been written that Mapplethorpe was an exacting traditionalist who might have been a sculptor rather than a photographer if he been born a century or two earlier. He worked in a documentary style, insisting on the formalism and the seriousness of the studio. With subject matter ranging from nude men and women to flowers to his own body, his work engaged the intellect rather than the libido.

"When you look at a Mapplethorpe nude, it hits you, consciously or subconsciously, that it does not work with the safety and control of a glossy photo of flesh. Instead, it feels as if you are close to a living body." (Jonathan Jones, *The Guardian*, 2010)

– Sarah J. McDonald

Joel Shapiro

This unique sculpture, *Untitled*, is said to be the representation of an angel allowing itself to be a carried away into space. The forms result from the artist's struggle to find a structure that reflects real psychological states, and thanks to the special treatment of their surfaces—which, through irregular lines and structures, suggest the texture of grain—they appear to be created from cut wood. This supports the impression of the sculpture's lightness while reinforcing an artisanal simplicity.

Joel Shapiro spent decades patiently exploring a geometrical sculptural language that is situated almost precisely at the intersection of the abstract and figurative. His work pursues a sort of vitality that floats in a state of suspended animation where there is often an allusion to the human figure.

When asked about his works' association with landscape or a figure, he replied, "I think artists are always inventing something, but it has reference to the world. It has reference to other artists, to art history. There is nothing entirely new. We all, more or less, have the same physiology, or the same intelligence, the same information, and you are working on problems that people have been addressing for thousands of years. So there is more in common between 19th, 20th, and 21st century sculpture than there is not in common. It is a language that is evolving." (Joshua Fischer, "New Installation: Interview with Joel Shapiro," *Temporary Art Review*, April 23, 2012)

Joel Shapiro creates a remarkable sense of movement from a seemingly stable figure. A result of that motion, the figure is transformed; where there once was weight, we now find miraculous motion.

– Sarah J. McDonald

Each of these works appropriates other imagery in order to comment on the idea of salvation. Tàpies incorporates the Christian symbol of the cross, while Currier references the imagery of Géricault's *The Raft of the Medusa*. How do Tàpies and Currier approach the issues of salvation and redemption? In their worlds, are salvation and redemption possible?

REDEMPTION

Antoni Tàpies *Esfera i Cadena*

Erin Currier *The Raft*

Antoni Tàpies

Antoni Tàpies is widely considered to be one of Europe's most important post-war artists. He was born in Barcelona in 1923, and his adolescence was disrupted by the Spanish Civil War. Tàpies addressed contemporary political and social issues, especially in relation to his Catalan heritage, and his early work was influenced by the art of Max Ernst, Paul Klee, and Joan Miró, as well as by Eastern philosophy.

Tàpies created his own language of signs and symbols, which often alluded to mysticism and spirituality. He studied the transformative qualities of matter—earth, stone, pieces of detritus—and expressed his ideas using different materials (latex, varnish, cardboard, collage) and techniques (graffiti, ballpoint pen, imprinting). Using these mediums, he was able to sustain his exploration of pictorial surfaces.

This sculpture was created late in the artist's life, perhaps as a symbol for contemplation. In *Artforum International*, Donald Kuspit wrote that "there are objects that reek of death and look to salvation, however ironically. The bronze orb of *Esfera i Cadena* (Ball and Chain), 1999 has a heavy chain attached, but the crucifix on top promises resurrection."

– Sarah J. McDonald

Erin Currier

World traveler Erin Currier's work crosses many boundaries, combining portraiture, collage, and sociopolitical commentary. Informed by Latin American muralist traditions, Eastern spiritual iconography, and social realism, her work incorporates consumer waste from more than three dozen countries to create an archival feast for viewers.

"The more I travel," says Currier, "the greater my sense of urgency as an artist to address social inequality and economic disparity through my work."

The Raft is a satirical commentary on the absurd treatment that travelers receive. The piece is an homage to Géricault's *The Raft of the Medusa*, for which she felt a great affinity. The composition and figures in *The Raft* mirror Géricault's original work, with a modern spin. Currier's version is made of trash collected from all over the world, and all of the materials in the background reference the story itself.

"On a political and philosophical level during Géricault's time," Currier explains, "ships were considered the crowning achievement of his home country of France. Ships were symbols of colonial power and imperialism. Today, airplanes are symbols of imperial power and might." Currier mocks the raft, poking fun at the notion that an inflatable device could protect humans from the elements. "Air travel puts you in such a vulnerable position with national boundaries. It's like sitting in your underwear," she observes.

The artist continues: "What began as a natural integration of my sociopolitical beliefs with a sheer joy of art-making has since developed into a full-fledged artistic praxis, by which I integrate the human realm I come in contact with in the course of my travels—its individuals, cultures, and struggles—with its refuse, in order to comment on and participate in the issues I feel most passionate about."

– James Burns

Using widely different mediums and aesthetics, each of these artists depicts July. Hurd creates a literal representation of the landscape that appeals to the senses, while Serra's version, full of movement, is an abstract reference to the month. How does texture in each piece contribute to the varying interpretations of a shared subject?

MEDIUM

Richard Serra *July #17*

Peter Hurd *The Month of July*

Richard Serra

Drawing provides a space, a place for me to go to where I can concentrate on an activity that is satisfying in and of itself.
—Richard Serra

Richard Serra is considered one of the most influential sculptors of the American post–Abstract Expressionist period. Working predominantly in Corten steel, he has influenced sculpture as we know it by challenging notions of scale, weight, and siting.

Serra has also been drawing since the 1970s, primarily using black paint stick. His drawings exponentially expand the definition of the genre by providing an intimate response to his public sculpture, while at the same time maintaining the same rigor and strength that inform those large-scale pieces.

In the series *July*, from 2011, the artist employs a primal and basic gesture of applying melted oil stick to handmade Japanese paper. The material is purposely left visible and palpably textural, so that it maintains (quite importantly) a three-dimensional volume.

When presented together, the *July* series has a beautiful dancing rhythm, a regular recurring motion, rich in symmetry. As an anonymous viewer put it in 1971, rhythm possesses a "movement marked by the regulated succession of strong and weak elements, or of opposite or different conditions."

When presented alone, the works are meditative, raising fundamental questions about the roles of sculpture versus drawing, and how the two can be combined and perfectly merged.

– Serena Cattaneo Adorno

Peter Hurd

A regionalist painter known for his landscape, figure, and genre paintings of New Mexico, Peter Hurd was especially focused on capturing light and atmosphere. Twelve of his paintings were published in *Arizona Highways*, depicting the months of the year. Each one highlights the area around the Hurd family ranch in San Patricio, New Mexico, in the Rio Hondo Valley, between Ruidoso and Roswell.

Describing this painting, published in the magazine's July 1972 issue, Hurd remarked: "The vertical contrast here between violent sky and tranquil fields is more dramatic than is visually evident as we view this picture, for we need to recall the longing with which we await the summer monsoon, the sweet dusty smell of rain long before a drop has fallen, and to remind ourselves that soon the runoff will be gullying out of the angry channel it has cut through these most exquisitely textured of all Hurd hills. The intense light on the bajadas above the rocky still-dry arroyo tells us that despite the storm, somewhere through some unseen rent beyond our vision, the sun still is strangely shining. The tiny figures of man and beast hurrying to finish the haying are dwarfed by this landscape, yet withal there is a warm sense of humanity here, doing commonplace things in an uncommon land."

Many of Hurd's works depict the panoramic views and people of his beloved ranch. He admired the sunlight in the region and the way it played upon the arid landscape. Exceptionally talented at capturing the colors and atmosphere of the Southwest, Hurd created paintings that almost emanate light, rather than merely depicting it, allowing viewers to immerse themselves in the environment.

– James Burns

The angular forms of these pieces demonstrate how movement in a work of art can be achieved through the use of line. The two paintings depict dance, yet there is also movement in Smith's piece, which could be compared to an aerial dance. How does line create motion, both two- and three-dimensionally?

MOTION

Emil Bisttram *Untitled (Indian Dancers)*

Kiki Smith *Back Porch Whispering*

Lloyd Moylan *Dance Movement*

Emil Bisttram

The following quote from Walt Wiggins' biography of Emil Bisttram, titled *The Transcendental Art of Emil Bisttram*, summarizes the artist and his approach to life and work so beautifully that it is presented as is.

"Over the years Bisttram's painting raged through stages of contradictory styles, from varying degrees of representationalism, expressionism, neo-classicism, cubism, realism, the metaphysical and many varieties of abstraction. He could paint the sacred fervor of a primitive Indian tribal dance in a potent modern style featuring animated gestures, bold rich colors and inventive composition to emphasize the living emotion of the ceremony; or could interpret the same ceremony in abstracted rhythmic patterns and robust design that evoke the spirit paralleling the ritual itself.

The same breadth of vision guided his life in a real sense, he made his life a work of art. Painter, muralist, philosopher, mystic, educator and public-minded intellectual, Bisttram was guided by an intense vision of the boundless growth potential of mankind through the understanding of the arts and their interrelationships. Early in his career he wrote:

Art concepts and all tangents therefrom are a matter of relative comprehension. It is my conviction that Art, for the artist and the layman, is a means to unfold the consciousness and thereby bring it to envision and experience wider horizons. Art, therefore, should concern itself not with imitation but with creation, otherwise it fails in its prime purpose: that of inspiring and stimulating thought. It brings to the life of the artist and to the layman an experience on a higher plane of emotion and intellectual perception without which there can be no real progress in man's development."

– Laura Finlay Smith

Kiki Smith

Since the beginning of the 1980s, Kiki Smith's work has consistently dealt with the theme of nature as it relates to the physical and psychological aspects of human beings.

Her father, Tony Smith, was a Minimalist artist known for his large polyhedron-based structures, and Smith and her sisters often spent time assembling paper models of his sculptures. From an early age, she was exposed to the art world: Abstract Expressionism and Minimalism, including significant contemporary artists Pollock, Rothko, and Newman. Smith's early experience in printmaking resulted in a fascination with recurring visual motifs. "I think there's a spiritual power in repetition," she has said, "a devotional quality, like saying rosaries."

The poetic, lyrical imagery in *Back Porch Whispering* evokes a sense memory of a back porch on a hot summer evening, with rocking chairs creaking on weathered wooden planks. The piece is reminiscent, too, of the back porch scene from the 1962 movie *To Kill a Mockingbird*, based on Harper Lee's book of the same name. There the viewer is preoccupied by the noises in the bushes, perhaps even hearing their own hearts beating at an insistent pace.

In an interview, Smith has stated that she prefers the concepts of her art be open to interpretation by the viewer. She added that ninety-nine percent of her work is psychological, which serves to widen the interpretation gap even further.

Take your position in the looking glass under *Back Porch Whispering*. Kiki Smith has delivered us a fable.

– Sarah J. McDonald

Lloyd Moylan

Prior to moving to New Mexico in the early 1930s, Lloyd Moylan taught art at the Broadmoor Academy, in Colorado Springs. A major figure in the New Deal art programs, he painted numerous murals throughout the Southwest and later became the curator of the Museum of Navajo Ceremonial Art, in Santa Fe, New Mexico. As a result, he incorporated into many of his paintings scenes of Native American dances and daily life.

Moylan's use of saturated color and loose, expressive brushstrokes appears to be informed by the Post-Impressionists and Fauvists, but he also explored modernist techniques such as Cubism, breaking objects into rudimentary spatial planes. *Dance Movement* not only demonstrates this latter technique but also shows how a strong sense of movement can be achieved through the use of line and shadow. As they perform a ceremonial dance with rattles and pine boughs in their hands, the three dancers in the piece are deep in concentration. However, when a viewer looks at their legs and feet, it may appear that there are more dancers in the scene than just three.

– Laura Finlay Smith

This pairing examines the iconography of the Madonna and Child, a theme that both Moore and Souza returned to time and again. This particular comparison is a natural one, since Souza's piece was painted in response to Henry Moore's sculpture, which is located at St. Matthew's Church in Northampton, England. What similarities do the two pieces share? How are they different?

MADONNA & CHILD

Henry Moore *Madonna and Child*

Francis Newton Souza *The Virgin of Northampton*

Henry Moore

From as early as the 1920s, the subject of the mother and child was a major theme in Henry Moore's work. In the two decades that followed, he began abstracting his forms, focusing on symbolism rather than attempting anatomical realism. Moore continued to explore the theme during World War II. In contrast to the scenes of terror and brutality that the artist witnessed by day, it was the visions of human sympathy and love expressed by the people who sheltered at night in the London Underground that imbued his own art with a newfound tenderness and maturity of style. That maturity is reflected in the 1943 sculpture *Madonna and Child*, commissioned for St. Matthew's Church in Northampton, England.

The maquettes created for the piece represent the artist's return to sculpture after the war years. One of the elements that defined a new conception of the mother and child is his treatment of drapery, which hangs in heavy folds between the knees. Here Moore reaches beyond modernism to refer back to classical Greco-Roman art and the Renaissance. However, contrary to these traditions, he abstracts his figures, stripping all unnecessary ornamentation from the composition, which results in a sculpture of timeless ambiguity.

On a high-backed chair (not unlike a throne), the Madonna sits upright, her knees bent, as she lovingly balances her infant on her knee. It was of utmost importance to Moore that his work be instilled with a human quality that spoke to people on a personal level, while also acting as a symbol that could transcend the boundaries of specific religions and cultures.

Despite its diminutive scale, the bronze was conceived as a monumental form, and a sense of grandeur can be seen in what became the final iteration of the work. This bronze was cast from one of eleven clay models and is one of two from the series that includes a formal seat—an element of classical majesty that, interestingly, Moore rejected in the final monumental version.

– Rob Dean

Francis Newton Souza

The subject of the *Madonna and Child* by Henry Moore, in the Church of St. Matthew's in Northampton, provided the direct inspiration for Francis Newton Souza's painting *The Virgin of Northampton*. The influence of Moore's sculpture on Souza is part of a much broader dialogue that occurred shortly after India gained its independence from Great Britain, in 1947. At the time of Francis Newton Souza's arrival in London, in 1949, Moore was already an influential artistic figure in England, and the influence of British artists like Moore and Francis Bacon on the early careers of Indian artists such as Souza and Tyeb Mehta is frequently overlooked or understated.

When considering Souza's decision to produce a painting based on Moore's sculpture of the same subject, it is particularly interesting to note that Moore was agnostic and expressed mixed feelings about modern ecclesiastical art. It is likely that his views would have appealed to Souza, who, despite having a Roman Catholic upbringing in Goa, remained deeply suspicious of the church and its religious leaders.

It may be that Souza recognized in Moore's sculpture a blend of artistic traditions that he admired. The syncretic approach that Moore chose, both in artistic and philosophical terms, reflected the approach that Souza had already subconsciously adopted in his own work. Hence, despite Souza's natural reluctance to be overtly influenced by any modern artist, his decision to pay homage to Moore's sculpture is a natural one.

It is interesting to note that in this piece, Souza has chosen to depict the Madonna in dark tones of brown and black, while the Christ child is rendered in pale tones. The intentional use of two opposing color schemes may symbolize Souza's experience of growing up as a Christian in a predominantly Hindu country. The black female figure, therefore, may in part represent Mother India and Souza's cultural roots, whilst the figure of the Christ child represents his Western faith—a duality of experience that was at the core of his entire artistic output.

– Rob Dean

Each of these pieces depicts Taos while showing contrasting aspects of the area. Kloss represents the natural landscape with mountains that eclipse the buildings below. Bernath, on the other hand, has focused on civilization. What do these two approaches say about the relationship between nature and culture?

ENVIRONMENT

Gene Kloss *Taos Scene*

Sandor Bernath *Untitled (Ranchos de Taos Church)*

Gene Kloss

By the time she first visited Taos on her honeymoon, in 1925, Gene Kloss had already established the beginnings of a distinguished art career in her native California.

Over the course of that career, which spanned seventy years, Kloss, a longtime member of the Taos art community, created paintings, watercolors, and a substantial number of etchings and aquatints—more than six hundred and twenty-five. She earned the respect of all the members of the occasionally contentious Taos Society of Artists as well as the national regard of her peers, who elected her to associate membership in the prestigious National Academy of Design in 1950 and full membership in 1972, making her the first American woman printmaker ever to be so honored.

The primary subject of her work was New Mexico, including the daily life of Taos Pueblo and ceremonies celebrated at various times of the year. Most compelling to Kloss, however, were the members of the pueblo, whose portraits she captured, and the high desert landscape itself, with its distinctive architecture and brilliant light.

— Laura Finlay Smith

Sandor Bernath

An artist whose primary medium was watercolor, Bernath was well regarded during the 1920s, 30s, and 40s for his distinct modernist style. Although he is primarily recognized for his scenes of marine life, his first trip to the Southwest, in 1935, left a strong impression on him, and he spent some very productive time in Taos.

This beautiful winter scene shows the iconic Ranchos de Taos Church (also known as the San Francisco de Asis Mission Church) standing guard as protector of the town, hushed and pristine after a big winter storm. While most inhabitants are nestled in their warm homes, a sole individual is traipsing across the plaza; this figure provides the viewer with a sense of perspective, as well as a sense of the grand scale of the imposing building, which has been depicted by numerous artists around the world. A beautiful sense of light and subtle detail throughout the painting add to its interest and depth, heightened by the use of crisp lines, geometric shapes, and a natural palette.

– Laura Finlay Smith

There are many similarities to be found between these two images: they are both dual portraits, the figures stare at the viewer, and the feeling of lethargy is palpable. Which elements in the pieces contribute to that particular mood?

MOOD

Alice Neel *The Black Boys*

Ketaki Sheth *Riddhi and Siddhi, in their living room, Norbury, London, 1997*

Alice Neel

Alice Neel was one of the great American painters of the 20th century. She possessed a classic concern for portraiture and painted in a style that was distinctly her own, creating works that were simultaneously intimate and revealing. The sitters' faces and body language are central to each work, yet there are often background details in the compositions that provide the viewer with more information about the subjects and their reactions to their surroundings. This dynamic is perfectly exemplified in *The Black Boys*. The frontality of the subjects and their penetrating looks set the stage for an exchange with the viewer; it is as though they are judging their creator and sharing those emotions directly.

Neel worked hard to move through the barriers of class in order to reveal the essential traits of her subjects. As the artist herself put it, "I have only become really known in the sixties because I could not defend myself. I read a quote from Simone de Beauvoir saying that no woman ever had a world view because she always lived in a man's world. For me this was not true. ... No matter what the rules are, when one is painting one creates ones own world. Injustice has no sex and one of the primary motives of my work was to reveal the inequalities and pressures as shown in the psychology of the people I painted." (*Alice Neel: The Woman and Her Work*, Georgia Museum of Art, 1975)

– Laura Finlay Smith

Ketaki Sheth

This portrait is from a body of work of twins from a single community, all with the last name Patel, shot in the United Kingdom and India between 1994 and1998. It was subsequently published as a book called *Twinspotting: Portraits of Patel Twins in Britain and India* (Dewi Lewis Publishing, UK, 1999, with a foreword by Raghubir Singh).

My idea was not to document the Patel community but rather to portray it in an iconic way. I began the process by searching out several generations of Patel twins, ranging from seventeen months to seventy-eight years; ultimately, I found and photographed one hundred such sets. The variance in light, season, workplace, and residence, both in India and the United Kingdom, offered me the latitude to contrast the differences that paradoxically reside in sameness.

Riddhi and Siddhi Patel, the eight-year-old twins pictured, lived in London with their parents and handicapped brother. Over the course of an afternoon, I photographed them in several situations at home. After a while, they grew restless and fidgety, as most children do. Then boredom set in. One twin threw off her shoes and socks, and both undid their neatly braided hair. The girls seemed more comfortable and natural in their disheveled states, and as inertia crept in, their attitudes seemed to say, "What's next? Please get on with it." It was then that I shot this image in their living room.

Between photographer and subject there comes a moment where everything just falls into place. And, often—as in this case—such a moment is not the result of a plan.

– Ketaki Sheth

Both of these works show how liquid can be used to create abstracted effects. Frankenthaler did it through the use of the medium itself; diluting the paint allowed her to create layered illusions on paper. Kertész's photograph exploits water's natural ability to distort the human figure. Although many viewers expect photographs to reflect "the truth," he provides an example of imagery that has been manipulated. How does visual distortion affect our view of reality?

DISTORTION

André **Kertész** *Underwater Swimmer, Esztergom*

Helen Frankenthaler *Untitled, 1980*

André Kertész

After I was wounded [in WWI] I was in the hospital for almost
nine months. We went swimming in the pool every day, and I
realized the distortions in the water. When I photographed them
my comrades said, "You are crazy. Why did you photograph
this?" I answered: "Why only girl friends? This also exists." So I
photographed my first distortion in 1917—others followed later,
especially the nudes in 1933.
– André Kertész, *Kertész on Kertész: A Self-Portrait*

Kertész is best known for his images of life's mysterious, nuanced,
and lyrical moments captured with a small camera, and his piece
Underwater Swimmer, Esztergom is somewhat more surreal than the
"real" images he is recognized for.

Taken at midday, with the harsh light forming scale-like patterns of
shadow and light in the pool, the photo depicts a swimmer appearing
like a headless sculpture, slicing the pool diagonally in two halves,
his sinewy body about to glide into the still, almost rippleless water.
Kertész has managed to capture the swimmer's slow dive just as his
head is submerged but before his feet touch the water. There is a zen-
like calm in the image and a silence that is palpable.

As John Szarkowski eloquently remarks in his book *Looking
at Photographs*, Kertész "loved the play between pattern and deep
space; the picture plane of his photographs is like a visual trampoline,
taut and resilient." His pictures evoke "a free and childlike pleasure in
the beauty of the world and the preciousness of sight."

– Ketaki Sheth

Helen Frankenthaler

In 1952, Helen Frankenthaler was giving rise to a new movement in American art—Color Field painting, which was marked by airy compositions that celebrated the joys of pure color. Frankenthaler pioneered what came to be known as a soak-stain technique, and she applied this breakthrough technique to other painterly media, most notably watered-down acrylic, which she used in place of turpentine-thinned paint starting in the 1960s.

Frankenthaler worked with paper as well as canvas, and used to pour her paint directly on the canvas, taking a very physical approach to creating art. The elements of Frankenthaler's paintings suggest parts of bodies and parts of landscapes—neither a body nor a landscape, but both at once. This piece expresses the luminosity of pure organic waves sweeping across the paper, which may be interpreted as the passage of time.

In *The Heroine Paint: After Frankenthaler* (Gagosian Gallery, 2015), Carrie Moyer wrote of the artist, "She talks a lot about how gestural painting with a brush is overly emotional or theatrical. She's not interested in showing us the narrative of how the painting got made—despite the interest in her process, everything seems to 'appear' in a painting all at once."

Recognized as one of the great American artists of the 20th century, Frankenthaler is quoted in John Gruen's 1972 book, *The Party's Over Now*, as saying, "I don't resent being a female painter. I don't exploit it. I paint."

– Sarah J. McDonald

Though they are separated by decades, these two works speak to each though their utilization of collages and their commentary on the nature of humanity and the issue of civil rights. How do the various references influence our understanding of each piece's subject matter?

ASSEMBLAGE

Lajos Vajda *Young Laborer*

Erin Currier *Friendly Skies*

Lajos Vajda

Lajos Vajda is considered one of the most distinctive artists of the Hungarian avant-garde movement. From 1927 to 1930, he studied at the Hungarian Academy of Fine Arts, and it was there that he—along with other like-minded students who shared his passion for modern art—established a group called Vadak (or "Wild Ones"). At this time, Vajda came into contact with poet and painter Lajos Kassák, a leading figure of the avant-garde and promoter of Hungarian Modernism.

At the end of the 1920s, Vajda developed a fascination with Russian Constructivism and socialist doctrine. He joined the Munka Kör ("Work Circle"), a collection of artists, intellectuals, and workers who shared a belief in an artistic renewal that was to coincide with societal revolution.

In his hometown of Szentendre, the artist recorded ideas to incorporate into his work, which juxtaposed religious symbols (both Jewish and Orthodox Christian) with architectural and folk art motifs, as well as abstract, figurative, and surrealistic elements. The resulting images were complex and visionary.

While traveling in Paris in the early 1930s, Vajda was introduced to Cubism and Surrealism. During this period, he also developed an appreciation for film and began creating photomontages depicting his fear of the impending fascist threat in his country. *Young Laborer* is one such piece. Against a repeating pattern created by traditional pottery jugs, Vajda has placed three male figures, each looking in a different direction. The largest in scale has a furrowed brow and a firmly set mouth. He looks away from the viewer—raising the issue of what exactly it is that he is contemplating. The viewer, therefore, is left not just with a sense of foreboding, but also with a question.

– Laura Finlay Smith

Erin Currier

Friendly Skies is part of a series of Erin Currier's work focusing on air travel. Currier deals thematically with the human struggle for equality and dignity, and during her travels in the years after 9/11, she has seen widespread airport discrimination against anyone who was Arab or Muslim (or both).

"It's a whole range of experiences, languages, and cultures, from very secular to very religious and very conservative to very liberal," Currier recalls. "There is a myriad of languages, races, and peoples. We have a very one-dimensional take in the United States on what it means to be Muslim." Currier tried to express that range of experience in this piece, using a Frida Kahlo painting, *On the Bus*, as compositional inspiration.

Friendly Skies also addresses classism. The work depicts an extremely wealthy man from one of the Arabian Gulf countries and a woman with a baby who looks like she is from a poorer country. Currier observes: "It's the classic 'blue-eyed capitalist versus peasant' dichotomy." Her intent was to depict a row of human beings. The viewer sees a group of people and then sees that they are Muslim and then sees that they are sitting on an airplane. The artist explains: "This is the reverse of the process that makes us first see 'the other.'"

While traveling, Currier constantly collects materials for her work, sometimes only understanding their significance after the fact. In *Friendly Skies*, behind the woman and child in the center, there is an Arabic-language newspaper, and the article featured cites millions of carnations floating in the sea. At the time Currier collected the paper, the story had no resonance, but later she heard a Palestinian journalist speak about the incident referred to in the article, in which Israelis dumped into the sea tons of carnations—the main crop of Palestine.

– James Burns

Each of these works depicts a wall. Scully found inspiration for his abstract paintings by viewing the ancient stone walls of the Maya people in Mexico, while Dusard found his inspiration in the man-made landscapes of mine quarries. Which elements in the two works reinforce (or contradict) our preconceptions about walls and what they symbolize?

WALLS

Jay Dusard *Wall, Abandoned Marble Quarry, Chiricahua Mountains*

Sean Scully *Wall of Light Pale Yellow Pink*

Jay Dusard

Vaqueros, buckaroos, and working cowboys have long been subjects of fascination for photographer Jay Dusard, who also maintains an interest in abstraction dating back to his days as an architecture student at the University of Florida.

Wall, Abandoned Marble Quarry, Chiricahua Mountains was taken in March 2012. A neighbor of Dusard's took him and a friend, fellow photographer Matt Cook, to a remote feature at the north end of the Chiricahua Mountains, the Arizona Marble Mining Company.

Recalling the trip, Dusard muses: "We drove up the old quarry road and hiked in for about three miles. I had two 4x5 cameras, one homemade and one view camera. I was struck by the slabs of marble littering the ground when I first saw the site. I made a vertical image with a 4x5 view camera with a falling front. I dropped the lens below the horizontal to get the rectilinear relationship true in the negative."

He took many images that day with this homemade 4x5 super-wide camera, shooting all of them from the rim of the quarry. Just as it was time to leave, Dusard decided to take a last-minute shot with the 4x5 view camera, and it turned out to be the only good negative of the day. He liked the way the light hit certain planes but not the main surface, which remained in the shade.

He recalls: "This image couldn't have been made at a more propitious time of day, and it couldn't have been done with a point-and-shoot camera." Dusard says that he "sees in black and white" and that "this wouldn't have been a great color subject. This image lends itself to black-and-white expression. It works best monochromatically."

– James Burns

Sean Scully

Sean Scully's *Wall of Light Pale Yellow Pink* is painted on Alu-Dibond, a composite material consisting of two sheets of aluminum sandwiching a polyethylene core. Looking for inspiration in a new medium, Scully worked with this innovative substance, which can be compared to the percussion section of a jazz band.

The broader concept of music implies repetition, bars, and notes of color, all elements visually reflected in this work. Interestingly, many theoretical works from the 18th century assigned emotional characteristics to different keys; for example, E major was seen as bright and piercing, and C major as completely pure. In *Wall of Light Pale Yellow Pink*, Scully clearly found his tone and rhythm. A master of mood, he drives his Irish soul through a storm, so to speak, allowing the viewer to witness the light beyond it.

The artist holds in admiration Manet and Velásquez for their lush black surfaces, Mark Rothko for his textured planes, and de Kooning for his brushstrokes. He has created photographs, watercolors, paintings, and sculpture employing what Kelly Grovier describes as "precisely that which has unsettled Scully's imagination over the course of his entire life and career: the conviction that freedom is a state we can only find if we never stop searching for it." (*Sean Scully, Different Places*, published by Chateau La Coste in association with the Kerlin Gallery, Dublin.)

– Sarah J. McDonald

Almost a century stands between these photos and this sculpture, yet ultimately Kläs' work is built upon the foundations of artists like Moholy-Nagy, who explored the simplicity of shape and line in order to construct a composition. Which compositional elements unite the work of Kläs and Moholy-Nagy? Which ones divide it?

COMPOSITION

László Moholy-Nagy *Konstruction*

Esther Kläs *Untitled (Come away with me)*

László Moholy-Nagy *Aluminiumbild*

László Moholy-Nagy

Moholy-Nagy, who taught at the Bauhaus in Germany between 1920 and 1933, began his career as a painter. By the mid-1920s, however, he thought of photography as the universal visual language of the modern era, because it was mechanical, impersonal, and objective, creating unexpected results.

The two works in this exhibition are "camera-less" photographs—works created without the use of a camera but with heavy reliance on paper, light, chemistry, and their maker's imagination. Moholy-Nagy and his first wife, Lucia, who was a photographer, experimented with this means of photographic expression to explore light and shade, transparency and form. While Moholy-Nagy was not the first to create this type of photograph, he coined the name for the technique.

In 1925, he published *Painting, Photography, Film*, a picture book that demonstrated the diverse possibilities in which photography challenged old ways of seeing—by showing very distant or very small things, for example, or by taking a perspective from above or below. The great majority of the illustrations were the work of scientists, journalists, and amateurs, not of artists. Moholy-Nagy's message was clear: photography had revolutionized modern vision without the aid of being termed art.

—Laura Finlay Smith

Esther Kläs

The sculptures of Esther Kläs have a ritual physical presence. The artist actually leaves traces of her physical work on the traditional materials she uses (such as wood), as well as the more industrial elements (such as resin and concrete).

"As in many of Kläs's sculptures, the cement retains the impressions of her fingers, indicating her close, physical relationship with the works." (*Art in America* review, March 2012.)

In *Untitled (Come away with me)*, Kläs deals with issues of confrontation and communication, the stillness associated with sculpture paradoxically eliciting the energy of movement and dialogue with the viewer. We can see that there is an empty space and an arm, perhaps, or a leg forming a pedestal where one could sit and converse. The protruding red monolithic structure would then talk about its belonging, its making, and its wanting.

There appears to be a soul within these forms, a vibrant energy that is set free, and it's no coincidence that included in Kläs' body of work are drawings that incorporate traces of movement, as in dance.

– Sarah J. McDonald

Taken together, these two works address the use of pattern, repetition, and color (or lack thereof), while also considering the issue of complexity versus simplicity. What are the effects on the viewer of rhythm and repetition in a piece?

RHYTHM

Christopher Wool *Untitled*

Jim Dine *Egypt in the Late 80s Early 90s*

Christopher Wool

Interpreting the paintings of Christopher Wool can be a laborious act. During the artist's first solo museum presentation in 1989, John Caldwell wrote of his pieces, "They are uniform, deliberate, absolute, and masterful, but entirely resistant to one's natural search for meaning, which they seem to deny."

Wool's compositions encompass abstraction via erasure, collage, and digital transformation, and *Untitled* arrived at a time when the artist added another technique in his evolving convergence of painting and process, the rubber stamp. It was then that Wool's compositions took on a tone of decorative imagery. This piece's repeating gate imagery involves an allover pattern, while also joining the individual stamped images to create the links in the gate.

Here we have a work specifically conceived for the medium, paper. It took many years—and assistance from a studio apprentice—for Wool to achieve mastery in handling the stencils, stamps, and alkyd.

Starting in the early 1970s, Wool lived and worked in New York, finding inspiration in the music of Ornette Coleman, who performed in SoHo, as well as in the work of filmmakers John Lurie and James Nares. After a brief period of film study at New York University, he served as a studio assistant for Joel Shapiro.

When painting came back on to the table, Wool was quoted as saying, "I became more interested in 'how to paint it' than 'what to paint.'"

– Sarah J. McDonald

Jim Dine

Jim Dine often uses everyday imagery and symbols in his art, such as tools, hands, and hearts. Although his pieces are not exactly characterized as Pop Art, their brilliant colors, repetition, and commonplace symbols reference Pop aesthetics. However, what truly separates Dine from the Pop Art movement is his keen attention to surface texture, which remains an important part of his work. In *Egypt in the Late 80s Early 90s* some colored squares seem to have been created by a series of washes, while others have thick impasto that rises off of the surface.

Dine's involvement with the art world began in the late 1950s with his participation in Happenings in New York. Around this time he also began to make assemblages that incorporated found objects. The concept of the everyday object continued into his paintings and prints, eventually becoming the staple of his art. Hearts are a regular feature in his work and serve as a repository for his emotions. Although their use is quite personal, the symbol is recognizable and relatable for the larger public.

In the early 1980s Dine began to explore imagery and symbols from ancient civilizations. This painting includes an Egyptian figure in the center. Because it has been left partially unfinished, its presence adds mystery to the work.

– Olivia Miller

Each a portrait of a single individual, these two works show how color can evoke a mood and even control the way the viewer understands the figure. In these two cases, the work becomes more about color than about the figure. What feelings or associations do the colors in each piece evoke?

EVOKE

Tyeb Mehta *Portrait of Husain*

William Eggleston *Untitled*

Tyeb Mehta

This painting, depicting the Indian artist Maqbool Fida Husain (pictured right), is a rare example of a portrait by Tyeb Mehta. The fact that Mehta chose to produce at least three portraits of Husain over his career is testament to the mutual admiration that the artists had for each other, both as people and as painters. Here, Tyeb has deconstructed the artist's face so that very few characteristic features of Husain's physiognomy remain, and yet the hooked nose, defined lips, and elongated fingers are elements that hint at his identity. The addition of a slim paint brush held in the artist's left hand is the final element leaving no doubt that it is the artist Husain being depicted.

In 1959, Mehta left India for England, where he lived for five years. Paintings from this period are influenced by European Expressionism and the work of post-war British modernists. The influence of Francis Bacon is especially notable during this period. Although the influence of Bacon's painterly style also remains faintly visible in Mehta's works of the early 1970s, by the middle of that decade, when this piece was produced, he had evolved his own method of paint application and deconstructive approach, both of which became characteristic of his mature style. The human figure remains a constant, while the potency of Tyeb's work lies in the balance of harmonious tones and lines within a deceptively simple composition.

"Mehta has been loyal to the human figure, recognizing man as always being at the centre of the universe. His art is that of the sensitive, contemplative, and mature individual, caught in the turmoil and pain of life but refusing to react to it with hysteria." (R. Hoskote, *Tyeb Mehta: Ideas Images and Exchanges*, New Delhi, 2005.)

– Rob Dean

William Eggleston

This photograph is from Eggleston's early work in Sumner, Mississippi, where he often lived with his grandparents as a young boy and where his grandfather introduced him to his first camera.

    We are looking at a young boy seated in a dimly lit room. Except for the orange glow of the lamp behind him and the pale orange upholstery of the armchair on which he sits, at first glance everything looks green—the drapes, the walls, the ceiling, the floor. Even the jacket reflects a paler shade of the drapes.

    There is something quite eerie, something strangely beautiful, about this boy relaxed in an armchair, his hands clasped in a heart shape above him, his gaze unaware of the photographer's. He is likely to be in his own home, if not in a home where he feels comfortable. To his left sits a woman—either his mother, aunt, or a visitor—with a glass in her hand, suggesting cocktail hour. Perhaps Eggleston is recalling his own youth in this image of the boy.

    Eggleston photographed in color at a time when so-called "real" art photography was all black and white. Though he captured the mundane and the familiar, his composition and palette always revealed a beauty in the everyday and banal. "I'm at war with the obvious," he once famously said of his work.

– Ketaki Sheth

These two works begin a conversation regarding the everyday in art. Themes of banality mix with thoughts of erasure, preservation, and memory. How do the pieces reflect the everyday? How do they use the everyday as a springboard for addressing something beyond it?

TRANSCENDENCE

Henri Cartier-Bresson *Mexico, 1963*

Robert Rauschenberg *Renovation*

Henri Cartier-Bresson

In this photograph, which is the wonderful opening image to Cartier-Bresson's book *Mexican Notebooks* (1995), a young girl is carrying a framed portrait, distressed at the edges, of a female bust, the head surrounded by a shaded haze. The tilt of the frame forms a diamond shape that shields the girl's torso; her head peeps out from the top, and her slender legs and unseen hands bear the framed burden, as she trots along a deserted Mexican street to a destination unknown to us. She appears unaware that someone has taken this picture of her.

The style and rendering of the portrait, the frayed edges of its frame, echo the past—something old and weathered. The child, in her vitality, symbolizes youth. Perhaps the portrait is of the girl's mother or her aunt or even her grandmother? This we will never know. What we do witness is fleeting memory and the passing of time.

True to his mastery of the decisive moment, Cartier-Bresson frames the image vertically between two corrugated fences, with an empty road receding into the background. In the foreground, the little girl takes a step, bearing the burden of a memory hidden from the viewer.

– Ketaki Sheth

Robert Rauschenberg

Robert Rauschenberg traveled frequently, amassing a wealth of experiences that he brought home with him to the United States. Through his art he generously shared what he saw, offering the American public an increased understanding of the political, economic, and humanitarian states of the countries he visited.

Not only did he incorporate simple objects and global images into his art, he was also open to all of the world's people. On a trip to the textile area of Ahmedabad, India, in the 1970s, for example, Rauschenberg gathered inspiration for several series. Inside a paper mill that had been established as an ashram, he worked with "soil"—a mixture of mud, paper pulp, ground tamarind seed, chalk powder, gum powder, and copper sulphate, all of which was mixed with water and kiln-fired.

Renovation, created in 1995, is part of a series called *Anagrams*. The artist was skilled in both printmaking techniques and image transfer, and he incorporated into this piece a water-soluble inkjet transfer process that enabled him to increase the scale of his paintings while creating subtle allusive effects.

These qualities can be seen in the blurry and dream-like *Renovation*. At the center of the painting is a cinderblock brick, a hammer, and other tools, along with the words "LOOK RIGHT"— all key ingredients necessary for repairing damage. On the right side of the painting, we see what could be a signpost signaling several directions to take, and on the left we see a Coke can, symbolizing America.

In 1961, the avant-garde composer John Cage wrote, "Beauty is now underfoot wherever we take the trouble to look." On his trip to India, Robert Rauschenberg most certainly found beauty underfoot and brought it to the surface for viewers to experience.

— Sarah J. McDonald

These two works explore the human figure while also abstracting it. Each figure defies its medium, whether stone or metal. How do those two hard materials capture (or distort) the qualities of soft flesh?

ABSTRACTION

Felipe Castañeda *Natura*

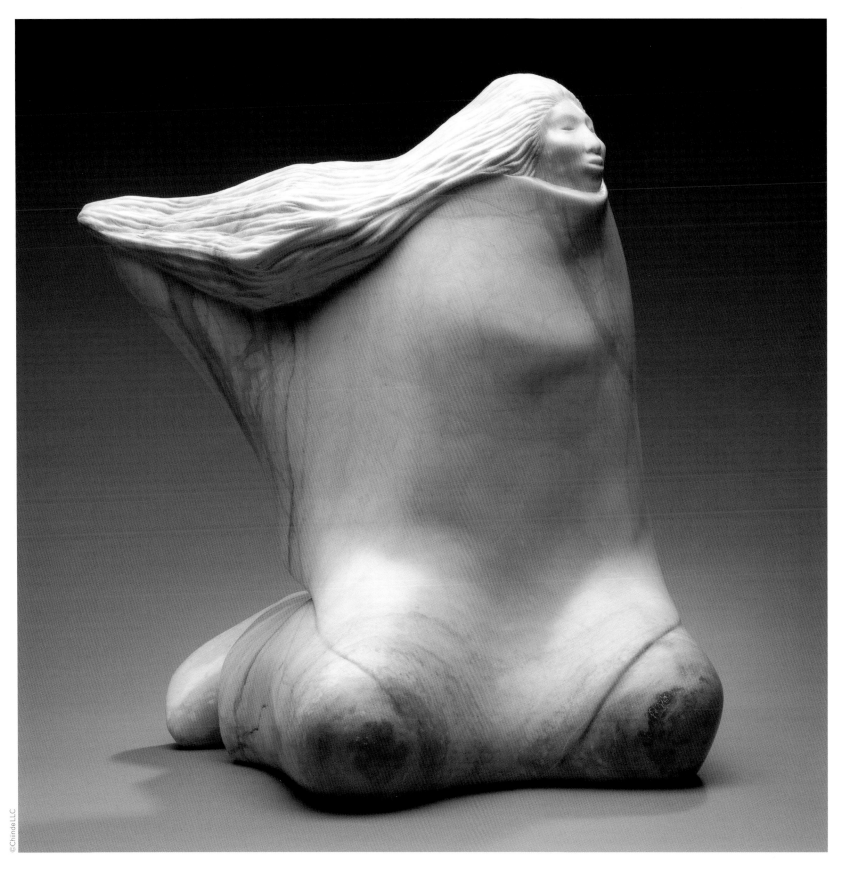

Allan Houser *Thinking of Him*

Felipe Castañeda

Felipe Castañeda's female forms embody the traditional and modern sensibilities of Mexico. Created from bronze and stone, these sculptural portrayals of motherhood and fertility evoke pre-Columbian culture while expressing a level of sensuality that is universal in its depiction of female beauty. Castañeda transforms his subjects' contemplative expressions and simple gestures into noble artistic ones, and the figures' perfect proportions demonstrate his deep knowledge of human anatomy.

Castañeda was born in La Paloma in the state of Michoacán, an area rich in pre-Columbian artifacts. As a young man, he moved to Mexico City to participate in the country's growing contemporary art scene. In 1958, he entered La Esmeralda Painting and Sculpture Academy of the National Institute of Fine Arts and began to develop a distinctive style in his approach to sculpture. He finished his studies in 1963 and worked hard to achieve his first major one-man show in 1970. Castañeda has since received numerous accolades in Mexico and elsewhere, and his work resides in private collections around the globe.

– Laura Finlay Smith

Allan Houser

A descendant of the Fort Sill survivors of the Warm Springs Chiricahua Apache, Allan Houser was born Allan Capron Haozous; the Apache name Haozous translates into English as "the sound of pulling roots." Grandson of the chief who served as Geronimo's interpreter (and a great-nephew of Geronimo himself), Houser was greatly influenced by his parents, who spoke their native language, sang, chanted traditional music, and recalled memories of Native American wars and struggles.

Houser decided to pursue a career in art, entering the Santa Fe Indian School at age twenty. Then-pioneering art instructor Dorothy Dunn encouraged students at the school to work in a traditional style, incorporating tribal identification in their subject matter to create historical-looking scenes. In his first year of enrollment, Houser was named the school's outstanding artist.

One of the most successful and influential Native American artists of the 20th century, Houser was renowned for his abstract Native subjects, such as *Thinking of Him*. He studied the work of modernists Jean Arp, Constantin Brâncuşi, Henry Moore, and Jacques Lipchitz, all of whom greatly influenced his work. Houser's sculptures were primarily created in stone, wood, and bronze; he created over one thousand during his career.

Appointed the head of the sculpture department of Santa Fe's Institute of American Indian Arts in 1962, Houser was instrumental in the advancement of indigenous art. While teaching, he continued to create sculpture, and it was then that he really began to integrate the aesthetics of the modernists with his own narrative ideas. During the late 1960s, as his work became more widely exhibited, recognition of Houser's unique style grew, as did his influence on students and other artists.

– James Burns

These two artists were teacher (Nordfeldt) and student (Jonson), and both took inspiration from New Mexico. Each of these images depicts an abstracted landscape. What is the relationship between land and sky in each one?

LANDSCAPE

B.J.O. Nordfeldt *Santa Fe Landscape (Talaya Peak)*

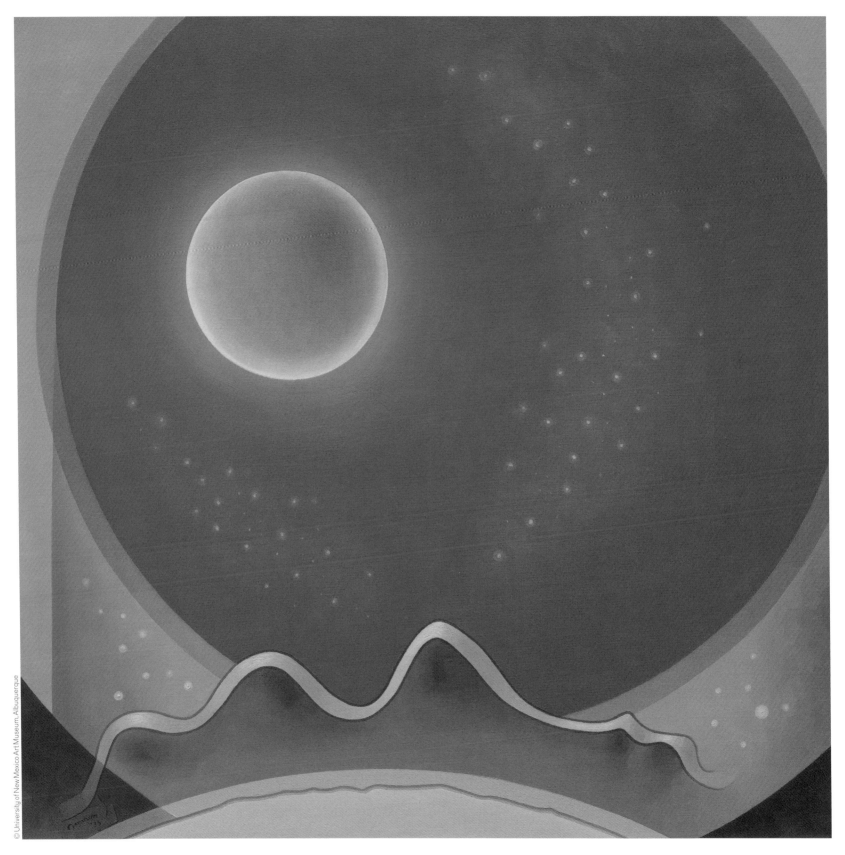

Raymond Jonson *Eclipse - Universe Series*

B.J.O. Nordfeldt

Nordfeldt, an early 20th century American modernist artist, was known for his abstracted, non-academic depictions of everyday subject matter. This stylized and distorted landscape depicts Talaya Peak (alternately known as Picacho), a prominent landmark on Santa Fe's horizon. It was painted just after Nordfeldt's arrival in Santa Fe in 1917.

A Swedish immigrant, Nordfeldt was influenced by the painting styles of Manet, Gauguin, and Cézanne whilst training in France. He was also enamored with the short-lived Fauvism movement, and his New Mexico paintings are particularly Fauvist-influenced. Fauvism is a French painting style created by a loosely formed group of early 20th century modern artists. Their works highlighted strong colors and embraced the medium in which the work was created, showing brush marks and texture rather than working to hide them.

An engraver and an etcher as well as an oil painter, Nordfeldt painted still lifes, portraits, and figures before turning to landscapes late in his career. An unusually early landscape for Nordfeldt, *Santa Fe Landscape (Talaya Peak)* is noteworthy for its strong use of color and its exploration of the relationship between land and sky. At the time of its creation, this work would have been stylistically shocking to many viewers.

Semi-abstract paintings became a hallmark of Nordfeldt's middle and late career. An austerity evolved in his style, in an effort to convey the significant. Interested in conveying the symbolic or emotional core of his subject, Nordfeldt employed techniques such as flattened forms and distorted space to create stylized images of his subjects. *Santa Fe Landscape (Talaya Peak)* is so laden with emotional power, it almost has a religious quality to it. For reasons unknown, Nordfeldt destroyed many of his landscapes prior to leaving New Mexico.

– James Burns

Raymond Jonson

Raymond Jonson took his formal training at the Chicago Academy of Fine Arts, where he studied under the great American painter B.J.O. Nordfeldt. "Nordfeldt's enthusiasm and vital spirit of experimentation had a genuine spark of what was then contemporary," Jonson said. "This he instilled in me through his work and conversation."

Jonson found his own work invigorated by the American Southwest—from the grandeur of the mountains to the brilliance of the light—and he moved permanently to New Mexico in 1924, but it was the early (and long-held) influence of avant-garde artist Wassily Kandinsky that served as his lodestar.

Eclipse - Universe Series perfectly exemplifies the ways in which Jonson took inspiration from the landscape while learning to impose his feelings on a scene and create interpretations of the things he saw. The space shown in the piece is the painting space, not a reproduction of a realistic one.

In 1938, Jonson, along with Emil Bisttram, founded the Transcendental Painting Group with an aim "to defend, validate, and promote abstract art." Ed Garman, a member of the group, wrote in his book, *The Art of Raymond Jonson, Painter*, "The *Universe Series*, begun in 1935, indicates that Jonson was indeed achieving a release from landlocked concepts. Long earthbound, the artist less into the cosmos. Rhythms develop in any and all directions. The paintings are open, airy, mysterious."

– Laura Finlay Smith

These four works are united through their incorporation of text in imagery. Each artist employs text in a unique way—for Ruscha the text is the image itself, while Twombly offers only the illusion of text. Lichtenstein and Williams use text aesthetically, while also allowing it to drive the narrative of the image. Are there other ways that text enables us to communicate beyond words?

Roy Lichtenstein *Sweet Dreams Baby!*

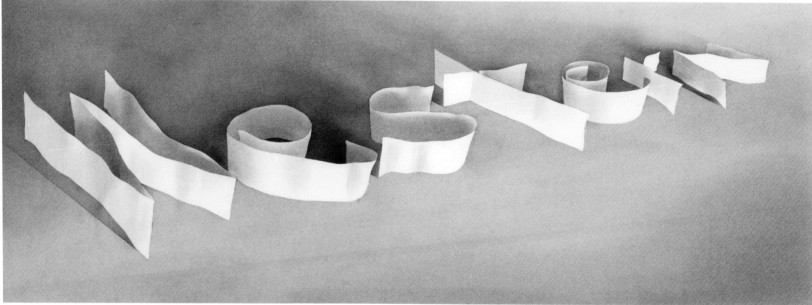

Ed Ruscha *Western*

Cy Twombly *Untitled (Ramification)*

Bernard Williams *Bass Reeves- Indian Territory*

Roy Lichtenstein

As one of the leading figures of the Pop Art movement, Roy Lichtenstein rose to the fore with his comic-inspired prints and paintings that featured his signature mark—the Benday dot. For this screenprint, as in many of his works, the text is essential to the understanding of the image. Apart from visually indicating the comic book likeness, the phrases also add or obscure meaning for the viewer.

The text in this image functions as a double entendre. The phrase "Sweet Dreams Baby" could be read in one of two ways—either as an endearing goodnight to a loved one or as a sarcastic and violent phrase. This dual meaning is appropriate, considering that Lichtenstein's art in general has presented many dichotomies, such as the difference between fine art versus commercial art and the mass-produced versus the handmade.

– Olivia Miller

Ed Ruscha

A wildly prolific artist, Ruscha has worked in photography, printmaking, painting, and even film. Since the 1950s, the written word has been a trademark of his work—sometimes incorporated to existing imagery and at other times, as in the case of *Western*, acting as the sole subject of the piece.

From his experience in commercial art, Ruscha developed a special fondness for words, often selecting them for their visual qualities rather than their meaning. His surroundings in Los Angeles, with its proliferation of advertisements and signs, have also proved to be a key influence for his work.

This work is an example of one of his "word excursions," where the text itself is the subject of the piece. Ruscha experimented with gunpowder as a medium, finding that it gave his art a unique texture and color. Although he used gunpowder in many drawings he made in the 1970s, the medium holds particular resonance for this work. Guns and the West go hand in hand; one can almost smell the smoking barrel.

– Olivia Miller

Cy Twombly

Scratches, scribbles, and drips proliferate in Cy Twombly's work. Though Twombly took great inspiration from other gestural artists like Willem de Kooning and Franz Kline, he developed his own signature marks. Travel to Morocco and Italy also proved to be a major influence, as it was in those countries that he came under the spell of tribal and classical art.

Twombly challenges the notion of artistic talent as being defined by naturalistic and realistic representation. At first glance, this work resembles a sheet of notebook paper. However, rather than depicting the paper in a realistic way, he implies its presence through the use of energetic blue lines and pencil-like scribbles. The childlike aesthetic of the markings, with their subtle blue lines, reminds the viewer of writing on paper, yet it is nonsensical. For Twombly, it was not so much about the line itself as it was about the experience making the line.

– Olivia Miller

Bernard Williams

Throughout his career Bernard Williams has worked in a variety of mediums, ranging from paintings to car sculptures. Much of his work comments on the intricate history of human relationships and the way events are recorded and remembered collectively. *Bass Reeves-Indian Territory* arranges words, symbols, and silhouetted figures in order to reflect on the complex history of the American West. The text in this painting is essential to understanding the artist's point. History is documented with the written word and catalogued in libraries and archives.

The written word has enormous power and is often taken as fact. For minority populations, this tendency has proved problematic, to say the least—in the written history of a nation, their stories are often misconstrued or neglected entirely.

Bass Reeves, one of the first black Deputy U.S. Marshals, was perhaps the original inspiration for the Lone Ranger figure. Reeves is often left out of the usual dialogue on the Western frontier, and Williams reminds us that the history of the West is complex, involving many interacting cultures.

– Olivia Miller

In the work of these two California artists, we observe the juxtaposition of tradition with experimentation. Corbett's intuition and freedom of gesture is contrasted with the more conventional approach of Dixon (who does, however, utilize a modern visual vocabulary). How does each piece represent a departure from a strict representational approach?

DEPARTURE

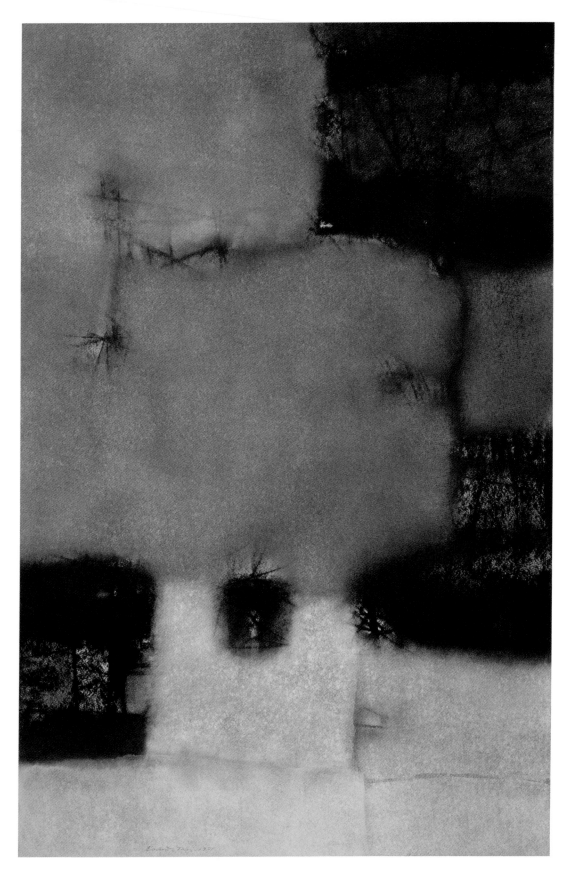

Edward Corbett *Number 10*

Maynard Dixon *Two Eagles*

Edward Corbett

Edward Corbett was included in the 1952 MOMA exhibition *15 Americans* as a result of the museum curator's trip to the University of New Mexico in Albuquerque to visit Richard Diebenkorn. She was there to consider his paintings for inclusion in the show, and Diebenkorn suggested that she also visit Corbett in Taos to see the pastels he was creating. Corbett was the only "new" artist chosen to participate in the show, which featured work by his friends Clyfford Still and Mark Rothko, along with Jackson Pollock, William Baziotes, and other well-established artists of the time.

Corbett and the Abstract Expressionists broke away from the realism and stylized abstraction that had dominated the American art world of the 1930s and early 40s. As Henry Niese noted in a 1979 exhibition catalogue, "Corbett rejected the notion of mere representation and directed himself to the larger goal of finding the formal framework in which he could express the fundamental beauty, mystery and meaning of nature to man in non-objective, and hence, more universal terms."

The drawings that Corbett completed while in Taos were works on paper using charcoal, chalk, pastel, and casein wash. By making marks, erasing, rubbing out, and correcting, the artist created a rhythm that resulted in soft abstracted forms, influenced by his love of the landscape and capturing the atmosphere so distinct to the region.

"I have a strong emotional attachment to the American Southwest—to the people and their culture, the language, the architecture, the food; but mainly I have an emotion about the landscape, the immense changing spaces of mountain and plain," Corbett said. "The emotion is important to my life as an artist. I believe my first moments of significant self-awareness of imaginative life were when I became speculatively involved with the dramatic nature around me." It was this fascination with the land that dominated Corbett's short-lived but brilliant career.

– Laura Finlay Smith

Maynard Dixon

Born in Fresno, California, in the San Joaquin Valley, Maynard Dixon began sketching at the age of ten. Frail health limited his childhood pastimes, but he sketched—a lot—and by the time he was sixteen he had the confidence to send his sketchbook to his hero, Frederic Remington. Encouragement and advice from Remington emboldened Dixon to enroll in art school in San Francisco at age eighteen.

Despite Remington's encouragement, Dixon dropped out of art school after only a few months. He roamed the Southwest and later found work as an illustrator in San Francisco. When the earthquake of 1906 destroyed his studio, he moved to New York City, where he became a noted illustrator. Dixon returned to the Southwest in the 1920s to paint scenes of the desert and execute a number of murals.

During his career, Dixon traveled extensively throughout the American West, painting and sketching. From these trips evolved his distinctive style: simplified shapes, dramatic forms, and clear and vivid colors, as seen in *Two Eagles*. This painting is typical of Dixon's stated desire to "interpret the vastness, the loneliness of the Western scene," and it demonstrates his reputation as a master of clouds.

Though Dixon was known as an illustrator, landscape painter, and muralist of the early 20th-century American West, the final two phases of his career, spanning the last twenty-five years of his life, position him as an early modernist painter who incorporated Post-Impressionism and Cubist-Realism into his landscapes and skyscapes.

Paul Bingham, Chairman of Thunderbird Foundation for the Arts, in Mt. Carmel, Utah, observes: "It is his uniquely modern style, one that gave the West a new language of expression, that makes Maynard Dixon's work so exciting."

– James Burns

Exhibition Checklist

JOHN BALDESSARI (American, born 1931)
Intersection Series: Landscape and Caravan (with Tall Tree)
2002
Digital photographic print and acrylic on sintra plate
72.38 x 64.88 in (183.8 x 164.8 cm) in four parts
MSPM JBA 01276

PROVENANCE
Sigrid Lorenz, Munich
Sprüth Magers, Berlin and London
The Tia Collection, 2011

EXHIBITED
Kunsthaus Graz am Landesmuseum Joanneum, Graz, Austria, *John Baldessari: Life's Balance: Werke 84-04*, March 5-May 16, 2005

ILLUSTRATED
Pakesch, Peter. *John Baldessari: Life's Balance: Werke 84-04*, Graz: Kunsthaus Graz am Landesmuseum Joanneum, 2005, p.182-83 (color)

Pages 7 and 27

SANDOR BERNATH (American, born Hungary, 1892-1984)
Untitled (Ranchos de Taos Church)
c.1940
Watercolor and pencil on paper
14 x 17 in (35.6 x 43.2 cm)
Signed lower right 'Sandor Bernath'

PROVENANCE
Dr. Ronald Bronitsky, Bernalillo, NM
Aaron Payne Fine Art, Santa Fe
The Tia Collection, 2015

Page 77

EMIL BISTTRAM (American, born Hungary, 1895-1976)
Untitled (Indian Dancers)
1936
Gouache on paper
23.25 x 19 in (59.1 x 48.3 cm)
Signed lower right 'BISTTRAM 36'

PROVENANCE
Robert Thebarge, Denver
David Cook Galleries, Denver, 2006
Private Collection, Chicago, 2008
David Cook Galleries, Denver
The Tia Collection, 2012

EXHIBITED
Desert Caballeros Western Museum, Wickenburg, AZ, *Sharing the West: The Tia Tradition*, May 24, 2014-March 14, 2015
Desert Caballeros Western Museum, Wickenburg, AZ, *Collecting the West: The Tia Collection*, November 2, 2013-March 2, 2014

ILLUSTRATED
Collecting the West: The Tia Collection, Wickenburg, AZ: Desert Caballeros Western Museum, 2013, p. 75 (color)

Page 64

LAVERNE NELSON BLACK (American, 1887-1938)
The Gathering
c.1920
Oil on canvas on board
16 x 24 in (40.6 x 60.9 cm)
Signed lower left 'LaVerne Nelson Black'

PROVENANCE
Private collection, c.1930
By descent in the family
Zaplin Lampert Gallery, Santa Fe
The Tia Collection, 2014

Page 34

ALEXANDER CALDER (American, 1898-1976)
La Botte (maquette)
c.1959
Sheet metal, rivets, gesso, black oil paint
19 x 18 x 11.5 in (48.3 x 45.7 x 29.2 cm)

PROVENANCE
The artist
Galerie Maeght, Paris
Dr. and Mrs. Blum, New York, 1989
Edward Tyler Nahem, New York
Dr. Martin L. and Francey Gecht, Chicago
Christie's, New York, *Post-War & Contemporary Art*, May 12, 2005, lot 248
Private collection
Gagosian Gallery, Paris
The Tia Collection, 2014

EXHIBITED
Galerie Maeght, Barcelona, *Calder*, February-March, 1989
Galerie Maeght, Paris, *Calder: Stabiles*, March 6-April 13, 1959

ILLUSTRATED
Baal-Teshuva, Jacob. *Calder 1898-1976*, Cologne: Taschen, 1998, p.54 (color)

NOTE
This work is registered as A11069 in the archives of the Calder Foundation. *La Botte* (maquette) is a scale model for a monumental sculpture of the same title, which is in the collection of the Museum Ludwig, in Cologne.

Page 9 and 46

T.C. CANNON (American, 1946-1978)
All the Tired Horses in the Sun
1971-72
Oil on canvas
42 x 42 in (106.68 x 106.68 cm)
Signed upper left verso 'T.C. Cannon'

PROVENANCE
The artist
Dr. and Mrs. Marvin Mones, Kensington, MD, 1972
By descent in the family
Zaplin Lampert Gallery, Santa Fe
The Tia Collection, 2012

EXHIBITED
National Collection of Fine Arts, Smithsonian Institution, Washington, D.C., April 7-May 29, 1972

LISTED
Adelyn Breeskin, *Two American Painters: Fritz Scholder and T.C. Cannon*, Washington, D.C.: The Smithsonian Institution Press, 1972, p.32

Page 33

HENRI CARTIER-BRESSON (French, 1908-2004)
Mexico, 1963 (printed c.1980)
Gelatin silver print
14.75 x 9.875 in (37.4 x 25 cm)
Signed in pencil, photographer copyright credit stamp verso

PROVENANCE
Henri Cartier-Bresson Foundation
Christie's, Paris, *100 Photographs from the Henri Cartier-Bresson Foundation*, November 11, 2011, lot 57
RDA, London
The Tia Collection, 2011

ILLUSTRATED
Cartier-Bresson, Henri. Fuentes, Carlos. *Henri Cartier-Bresson: Mexican Notebooks, 1934-1964*, London: Thames & Hudson, Ltd., 1995, p.13
Cartier-Bresson, Henri. Bonnefoy, Yves. *Henri Cartier-Bresson: Photographer*, Lausanne: Robert Delpire for the International Center for Photography, 1979

Page 124

FELIPE CASTAÑEDA (Mexican, born 1933)
Natura
2001
Bronze
Edition P/A of VII
26 x 24 x 24 in (58.42 x 30.48 x 60.96 cm)
Signed 'F. Casteñeda' on bottom of left foot

PROVENANCE
The artist
Nedra Matteucci Galleries, Santa Fe
The Tia Collection, 2009

EXHIBITION
Nedra Matteucci Galleries, Santa Fe, *Felipe Castañeda and Julian Robles*, June 27-July 18, 2009

Page 130

EDWARD CORBETT (American, 1919-1971)
Number 10
1951
Chalk and casein on paper
34.75 x 22.75 in (88.3 x 57.5 cm)
Signed and dated lower left 'Corbett-Taos-1951'

PROVENANCE
The artist
La Galeria Escondido, Taos
Mrs. Phillip Riskind, Chicago, 1952
By descent to Kenneth and Judith Riskind, Tucson
Aaron Payne Fine Art, Santa Fe
The Tia Collection, 2014

EXHIBITED
Museum of Modern Art, New York, 15 Americans, April 10-July 6, 1952

LISTED
15 Americans, New York: Museum of Modern Art, March, 1952, p.45

Page 150

ERIN CURRIER (American, born 1975)
Friendly Skies
2010
Mixed-media collage and acrylic paint on panel
36 x 48 in (91.4 x 121.9 cm)
Signed lower right 'Erin'

PROVENANCE
The artist
Blue Rain Gallery, Santa Fe
The Tia Collection, 2010

EXHIBITED
Blue Rain Gallery, Santa Fe, *Friendly Skies*, September 1-18, 2010

ILLUSTRATED
The Paintings of Erin Currier, New Mexico: CSF Publishing, 2011, p.28-29 (color)

Page 95

ERIN CURRIER (American, born 1975)
The Raft
2010
Mixed-media collage and acrylic paint on panel
60 x 72 in (152.5 x 182.9 cm)
Signed lower right 'Erin'

PROVENANCE
The artist
Blue Rain Gallery, Santa Fe
The Tia Collection, 2010

EXHIBITED
Blue Rain Gallery, Santa Fe, *Friendly Skies*, September 1-18, 2010

ILLUSTRATED
The Paintings of Erin Currier, New Mexico: CSF Publishing, 2011, p.48-49 (color)

Pages 9 and 53

RANDALL DAVEY (American, 1887-1964)
Untitled (Horse & Rider)
c.1950
Bronze
16 x 16.75 x 5.5 in (40.64 x 42.5 x 13.97 cm)
Signed next to rear left hoof 'R. DAVEY'

PROVENANCE
Private collection
Nedra Matteucci Galleries, Santa Fe
The Tia Collection, 2012

EXHIBITED
Desert Caballeros Western Museum, Wickenburg, AZ, *Collecting the West: The Tia Collection*, November 2, 2013-March 2, 2014
Brookgreen Gardens, Murrells Inlet, SC, *The Wild West in American Art*, May 5-July 29, 2012

ILLUSTRATED
Collecting the West: The Tia Collection, Wickenburg, AZ: Desert Caballeros Western Museum, 2013, p. 79 (color)

Page 32

JIM DINE (American, born 1935)
Egypt in the Late 80s Early 90s
1993
Oil on canvas
53 x 87.75 in (135 x 221 cm)
Signed, dated, and titled on verso 'Jim Dine 1993
Egypt in the Late 80s Early 90s'

PROVENANCE
The artist
Private collection
Société Sarl Claude Bernard, Paris, 2011
Galleria d'Arte Contini, Venice, Italy
The Tia Collection, 2013

Page 113

MAYNARD DIXON (American, 1875-1946)
Two Eagles
1932
Oil on canvas
30 x 40 in (76.2 x 101.6 cm)
Signed and dated lower left 'MAYNARD DIXON 1933'
Copyright symbol in red paint lower left corner
Titled verso in artist's hand 'Two EAGLES'

PROVENANCE
The artist
Edith Hamlin
John Howell Books, San Francisco
Senator Barry Goldwater, Phoenix
By descent in the Goldwater family, Phoenix
Gail and Neal Elliott, Gig Harbor, WA
David Cook Galleries, Denver
The Tia Collection, 2013

EXHIBITED
California Academy of Sciences, San Francisco, *Maynard Dixon: Images of the Native American*, June 18-October 18, 1981
Phoenix Art Museum, Phoenix, *Maynard Dixon Retrospective*, April 27-June 7, 1970
M.H. de Young Museum, San Francisco, *Maynard Dixon: Painter of the West*, August 24-October 6, 1968
Rotunda Gallery, San Francisco, *Paintings and Drawings by the Late Maynard Dixon*, January 22-February 8, 1953
San Diego Fine Arts Gallery, 1938
Frank C. Orr Gallery, San Diego, *Paintings by Maynard Dixon*, 1935

ILLUSTRATED
Maynard Dixon: Images of the Native American, San Francisco: California Academy of Sciences, 1981, p.59 (color)
Four Winds, Winter, 1981
Arizona Daily Star, February, 1941
San Diego Union, August, 1938

Page 151

JOELLYN DUESBERRY (American, born 1944)
New Mexico, Red Earth
2013
Acrylic on canvas
40 x 40 in (101.6 x 101.6 cm)
Signed lower right 'JTD'

PROVENANCE
The artist
Desert Caballeros Western Art Museum, *10th Annual Cowgirl Up! Art from the Other Half of the West*
The Tia Collection, 2015

EXHIBITED
Desert Caballeros Western Art Museum, Wickenburg, AZ, *10th Annual Cowgirl Up! Art from the Other Half of the West*, March 20-May 3, 2015

ILLUSTRATED
10th Annual Cowgirl Up! Art from the Other Half of the West, Wickenburg, AZ: Desert Caballeros Western Art Museum, 2015, p.16 (color)

Page 21 and front cover

JAY DUSARD (American, born 1937)
Wall, Abandoned Marble Quarry, Chiricahua Mountains
2012 (printed 2013)
Archival pigment (inkjet) print
38 x 31 in (96.5 x 78.7 cm)
Signed and dated lower right 'Jay Dusard 2013'

PROVENANCE
The artist
Phoenix Art Museum, *The West Select*
The Tia Collection, 2013

EXHIBITED
Phoenix Art Museum, Phoenix, *The West Select*, November 8-December 31, 2013

Page 100

WILLIAM EGGLESTON (American, born 1939)
Untitled
1970 (printed 2012)
Pigment print
Edition 1 of 2
Image size: 47.75 x 32.75 in (121.28 x 83.18 cm)
Signed, Eggleston Artistic Trust ©, on verso

PROVENANCE
The Eggleston Artistic Trust
Christie's, New York, *Photographic Masterworks of William Eggleston*, March 2012, lot 29
The Tia Collection, 2012

ILLUSTRATED
Spoon, *Transference*, Merge Records, 2010, record album cover (color)
Moore, Kevin. *Starburst: Color Photography in America 1970-1980*, Berlin: Hatje Cantz, 2010, p.9 (color)
Sussman, Elizabeth. *William Eggleston: Democratic Camera, Photographs and Video, 1961-2008*, New York: Whitney Museum of Art, 2008, (another example) p.58, pl.16 (color)
Szarkrowski, John. *William Eggleston's Guide*, New York: The Museum of Modern Art, 1976, p.92 (color)

Page 119

NICOLAI FECHIN (American, born Russia. 1881-1955)
Winter Landscape, Taos
c.1927
Oil on canvas
15 x 24 in (38.1 x 60.9 cm)
Signed lower left 'N. Fechin'

PROVENANCE
Mr. and Mrs. William Foxley, Denver
Gerald Peters Gallery, Santa Fe, 1997
Private collection, 1998
Nedra Matteucci Galleries, Santa Fe
The Tia Collection, 2009

EXHIBITED
Desert Caballeros Western Art Museum, Wickenburg, AZ, *Sharing the West: The Tia Tradition*, May 2, 2014-March 14, 2015
Desert Caballeros Western Art Museum, Wickenburg, AZ, *Collecting the West: The Tia Collection*, November 2, 2013-March 2, 2014
The Museum of Russian Art, Minneapolis, *Discovering 20th Century Masters: Nicolai Fechin*, August 25, 2012-January 20, 2013
Frye Art Museum, Seattle, *Nicolai Fechin*, February 9-May 19, 2013
Foundation for International Arts and Education, Bethesda, MD, *Nicolai Fechin: From Kazan to Taos* in the following locations:
State Museum of Fine Arts of the Republic of Tartarstan, Kazan, Russia, November 2, 2011-January 15, 2012
The Russian Museum, St. Petersburg, February 24-May 16, 2012
The State Tretyakov Gallery, Moscow, May 22-July 29, 2012
Gerald Peters Gallery, Santa Fe, *Nicolai Fechin: Across Two Continents*, October 17-November 24, 1997

ILLUSTRATED
Collecting the West: The Tia Collection, Wickenburg, AZ: Desert Caballeros Western Art Museum, 2013 p.91 (color)
Danzker, JoAnne Birnie. *Nicolai Fechin*, Seattle: Frye Art Museum, 2013, p.62 (color)
Nicolai Fechin: From Kazan to Taos, Bethesda: Foundation for International Arts and Education, supplement, 2012, p.38 (color)
Tuluzakova, Galina P. *Nikolai Fechin the Art and the Life*, Taos, Fechin Art Reproductions, 2012, p.386 (color)
Tuluzakova, Galina P. *Nikolai Fechin* (in Russian), St. Petersburg, Russia, 2007, pl.188 (color)
Across Two Continents, Santa Fe: Gerald Peters Gallery, 1997, pl.10 (color)

LISTED
Across Two Continents, Santa Fe: Gerald Peters Gallery, 1997

Page 41

HELEN FRANKENTHALER (American, 1928-2011)
Untitled
1980
Acrylic on paper
19.6 x 27.8 in (49.8 x 70.5 cm)
Signed and dated lower right 'frankenthaler 30 June, 1980'

PROVENANCE
Helen Frankenthaler Foundation, New York (FRANK 1980.0001)
Gagosian Gallery, London
The Tia Collection, 2014

EXHIBITED
Frieze Masters, London, October 16-19, 2014

Page 89

LEE FRIEDLANDER (American, born 1934)
New York City
2011 (printed 2012)
Gelatin silver print
Image size: 18.375 x 12.25 in (46.6 x 31.1 cm)
Paper size: 20 x 16 in (50.8 x 40.64 cm)
Signed, titled, and dated on verso in pencil, stamped verso in ink

PROVENANCE
The artist
Fraenkel Gallery, San Francisco
The Tia Collection, 2013

ILLUSTRATED
Friedlander, Lee. *Lee Friedlander: Mannequin*, San Francisco: Fraenkel Gallery, 2012, pl.94 and cover

Page 26

ALLAN HOUSER (American, 1914-1994)
Thinking of Him
1980
Alabaster
19 x 20 x 14 in (48.26 x 50.8 x 35.56 cm)
Signed on the edge of robe covering heel in rear
'Allan Houser'

PROVENANCE
The artist
Allan Houser Gallery, Santa Fe
The Tia Collection, 2013

EXHIBITED
Gilcrease Museum, University of Tulsa, Tulsa, *Form and Line: Allan Houser's Sculptures and Drawings*, February 13, 2014-June 29, 2015

ILLUSTRATED
Rushing III, W. Jackson. *Allan Houser: An American Master*, New York: Harry N. Abrams, Inc., 2004, p.192 (color)
Perlman, Barbara H. *Allan Houser*, Boston: David R. Godine, 1987, p.38-39 (color)

Pages 6 and 131

PETER HURD (American, 1904-1984)
The Month of July
c.1962
Egg tempera on panel
45 x 40 in (114.3 x 101.6 cm)
Signed lower left 'PETER HURD'

PROVENANCE
The artist
Pat, Tim, and Joe Leonard, Security National Bank, Roswell, NM
Nedra Matteucci Galleries, Santa Fe, 1994
Private collection, CA
Nedra Matteucci Galleries, Santa Fe
The Tia Collection, 2012

EXHIBITED
Desert Caballeros Western Art Museum, Wickenburg, AZ, *Sharing the West: The Tia Tradition*, May 2, 2014-March 14, 2015
Desert Caballeros Western Art Museum, Wickenburg, AZ, *Collecting the West: The Tia Collection*, November 2, 2013-March 2, 2014

ILLUSTRATED
Collecting the West: The Tia Collection, Wickenburg, AZ: Desert Caballeros Western
Art Museum, 2013, p.95 (color)
Holiday Newsletter, Santa Fe: Nedra Matteucci Galleries, 1995
Arizona Highways, Vol.XLVII, No.11, November 1972, p.24 (color)

Page 59

RAYMOND JONSON (American, 1891-1982)
Eclipse - Universe Series
1935
Oil on canvas
40 x 41 in (101.6 x 104.14 cm)
Titled, signed, and dated on original cardboard backing
fragment mounted on verso 'ECLIPSE-UNIVERSE SERIES
JONSON OIL 1935 40 X 41'
Titled, signed, and dated on label on cardboard 'ECLIPSE-
UNIVERSE SERIES JONSON 1935'

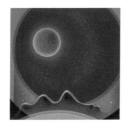

PROVENANCE
The artist
Gifted to the Salt Lake City Art Center Permanent Collection, 1970
Christie's, New York, *American Paintings*, May 23, 1990, Lot 237
Private collection, Houston
Nedra Matteucci Galleries, Santa Fe
The Tia Collection, 2015

Page 137

ANDRÉ KERTÉSZ (American, born Hungary. 1894-1985)
Underwater Swimmer, Esztergom
1917 (printed 1960)
Gelatin silver print
8 x 10 in (20.5 x 25.2 cm)
Signed in pencil on verso 'A Kertesz'
Hungarian cultural stamp on verso

PROVENANCE
Gallery Erdész, Hungary
The Tia Collection, 2012

EXHIBITED
The J. Paul Getty Museum, Los Angeles, *In Focus: Play*, December 23, 2014-May 10,
2015 (another example)
The J. Paul Getty Museum, Los Angeles, *André Kertész Photographs: Seven Decades*,
December 18, 2007-April 13, 2008 (another example)
The J. Paul Getty Museum, Los Angeles, *Photographers of Genius*, March 16-July 25,
2004 (another example)
The J. Paul Getty Museum, Malibu, *André Kertész: A Centennial Tribute*, June
28-September 4, 1994 (another example)

ILLUSTRATED
Clarke, David. *Water and Art*, London: Reaktion Books, 2010, p.69 (another example)
Naef, Weston. *Photographers of Genius* at the Getty, Los Angeles: The Getty
Museum, 2004, p.104, 105 (another example)

Page 88

ESTHER KLÄS (German, born 1981)
Untitled (Come away with me)
2009
Aquaresin, pigments, wood, concrete
50.75 x 52.375 x 50 in (128.9 x 127.9 x 127 cm)

PROVENANCE
The artist
Yvon Lambert Gallery, Paris
The Tia Collection, 2013

EXHIBITED
Yvon Lambert, New York, *A Stone Left Unturned*, February 1-March 9, 2013
Bureau, New York, *Opossums Persimmons: Nancy de Holl & Esther Kläs*, February
27-March 27, 2011

Page 107 and front cover

GENE KLOSS (American, 1903-1996)
Taos Scene
c.1938
Watercolor on paper
12 x 18 in (30.48 x 45.72 cm)
Signed lower right 'Gene Kloss'

PROVENANCE
Private collection, 1995
Private collection, Albuquerque, 1996
Zaplin Lampert Gallery, Santa Fe, 2005
Private collection, CA, 2005
Zaplin Lampert Gallery, Santa Fe
The Tia Collection, 2015

Page 76

ROY LICHTENSTEIN (American, 1923-1997)
Sweet Dreams Baby!
1965
Edition 129 of 200
Screenprint on white wove paper
38 x 28 in (96.5 x 71.12 cm)
Numbered in pencil lower left '129/200'
Signed lower right 'Lichtenstein'

PROVENANCE
Private collection
DTR Modern Galleries, Boston
The Tia Collection, 2011

Page 142

ROBERT MAPPLETHORPE (American, 1946-1989)
Phillip Prioleau
1979
Gelatin silver print
A/P 2/2
16 x 20 in (40.6 x 50.8 cm)
(MAP 342, RMP 1280)

PROVENANCE
Estate of Robert Mapplethorpe
Galerie Thaddaeus Ropac, Paris
The Tia Collection, 2015

EXHIBITED
Galerie Thaddaeus Ropac, Paris, *Robert Mapplethorpe*, curated by Isabelle Huppert, 2014
Galerie Thaddaeus Ropac, Salzburg, *Robert Mapplethorpe*, curated by Isabelle Huppert, 2013

ILLUSTRATED
Morrisroe, Patricia. *Mapplethorpe: A Biography*, New York: Random House, 1995, unpaginated, ill. after p.272 (another example)
Holborn, Mark. Levas, Dimitri. *Mapplethorpe*, London: Jonathan Cape, 1992, pl.161 (another example)
Takano, Ikuroh. *Robert Mapplethorpe*, Tokyo: Parco Co., 1987, un-paginated (another example)
Mapplethorpe, Robert. Shange, Ntozake. *The Black Book*, New York: St. Martin's Press, 1986, p.37 (another example)
Mapplethorpe, Robert. *Robert Mapplethorpe 1970-1983*, The Institute of Contemporary Arts, 1983, p.41 (another example)
Mapplethorpe, Robert. *Black Males*, Amsterdam: Galerie Jurka, 1980, p.32 (another example)

Page 47

TYEB MEHTA (Indian, 1925-2009)
Portrait of Husain
1975
Oil on canvas
44 x 35.5 in (112 x 90 cm)
Signed and dated on verso 'Tyeb 75' along with inscription 'Sakina'

PROVENANCE
The artist
Maqbool Fida Husain, Mumbai
Vadehra Art Gallery, New Delhi and London
Glenbarra Art Museum, Himeji, Japan
Sovereign FZE, Dubai
RDA, London
The Tia Collection, 2010

ILLUSTRATED
Hoskote, Ranjit. *Tyeb Mehta: Ideas Images Exchanges*, New Delhi: Vadhera Art Gallery, 2005, p.124 (color)

Page 118 and front cover

LÁSZLÓ MOHOLY-NAGY (Hungarian, 1895-1946)
Aluminiumbild
1926
Vintage gelatin silver print (photogram)
6 x 4.5 in (15 x 11.5 cm)
Signed, titled, and dated on verso 'Moholy Nagy, Aluminiumbild, glas creus, 1926'
Hungarian cultural stamp on verso

PROVENANCE
Moholy-Nagy Foundation
Gallery Erdész, Szentendre, Hungary
The Tia Collection, 2012

EXHIBITED
Gallery of Paks, Tolnai, Hungary, *Glass Architecture*, September 23-November 6, 2011

Page 108

LÁSZLÓ MOHOLY-NAGY (Hungarian, 1895-1946)
Konstruction
1923
Vintage gelatin silver print (photogram)
4.81 x 6 in (12.2 x 15 cm)
Signed, titled and dated on verso 'Moholy-Nagy, Konstruction, 1923'
Hungarian cultural stamp on verso

PROVENANCE
Moholy-Nagy Foundation
Gallery Erdész, Szentendre, Hungary
The Tia Collection, 2012

EXHIBITED
Gallery of Paks, Tolnai, Hungary, *Glass Architecture*, September 23-November 6, 2011

Page 106

HENRY MOORE (British, 1898-1986)
Madonna and Child
1943
Bronze
Edition of 7
5.88 x 3 in (15 x 7.5 cm)
LH221

PROVENANCE
The artist
By descent to his daughter, Mary Moore
Artcurial Briest-Poulain-F. Tajan, Paris, 2007
RDA, London
The Tia Collection, 2012

EXHIBITED
Henry Moore Intime in the following locations:
The Oita Prefectural Museum of Art, Oita, Japan, June 25-August 8, 1993
Hiroshima City Museum of Art, Hiroshima, Japan, April 9-May 16, 1993
Municipal Museum of Art, Kitakyshu, Japan, November 21-January 24, 1993
Sezon Museum of Modern Art, Karuizawa, Japan, September 15-November 3, 1992
Didier Imbert Fine Art, Paris, April 3-July 24, 1992

ILLUSTRATED
Sylvester, David (ed.), *Henry Moore Complete Sculpture*, Volume 1, London: Lund Humphries, Ltd., 1957, p.221 (The terracotta version of this bronze is illustrated)

Page 70

LLOYD MOYLAN (American, 1893-1963)
Dance Movement
c.1950
Watercolor on paper
28 x 34 in (71.1 x 86.36 cm)
Signed lower right 'L. Moylan'

PROVENANCE
Private collection, Santa Fe
Zaplin Lampert Gallery, Santa Fe, 1995
Mr. and Mrs. Paul Cahn, St. Louis
Zaplin Lampert Gallery, Santa Fe
The Tia Collection, 2012

EXHIBITED
Desert Caballeros Western Museum, Wickenburg, AZ, *Collecting the West: The Tia Collection*, November 2, 2013-March 2, 2014

Museum of New Mexico exhibition in the following locations: 1950: Tucumcari, Nov 12-25; Silver City, Dec 10-24. 1951: Albuquerque, Jan 7-21; Portales, Feb 11-25; Carlsbad, March 18-April 1; Lubbock, TX, May 17-June 1; Alamogordo, Nov 1-15; Alpine, TX, Dec 2-16. 1952: Socorro, Jan 6-20; Gallup, Feb 3-17; Clovis, March 12-22; Los Alamos, March 30-April 11

ILLUSTRATED
Collecting the West: The Tia Collection, Wickenburg, AZ: Desert Caballeros Western Museum, 2013, p.73 (color)

Page 66

WILLARD NASH (American, 1898-1943)
Springtime, Santa Fe
c.1920
Oil on canvas
20 x 24 in (50.8 x 61 cm)
Signed lower right 'Willard Nash'

PROVENANCE
Private collection, Santa Fe
Owings-Dewey Fine Art, Santa Fe
Jack and Mary Jo Harrod, Plano, TX
Private collection, Aspen, CO
Aaron Payne Fine Art, Santa Fe
The Tia Collection, 2013

EXHIBITED
Detroit Institute of Art, Detroit, *Annual Exhibitions for Michigan Artists Under the Auspices of the Scarab Club*, February 2-28, 1925

Page 40

ALICE NEEL (American, 1900-1984)
The Black Boys
1967
Oil on canvas
46 x 40 in (116.8 x 101 cm)
Signed and dated lower right 'Neel '67'

PROVENANCE
The artist
Private collection, 1979
Megan Fox Kelly, New York
The Tia Collection, 2011

Pages 5 and 82

B.J.O. NORDFELDT (American, born Sweden. 1878-1955)
Santa Fe Landscape (Talaya Peak)
c.1918-19
Oil on canvas
30 x 37.5 in (73.66 x 91.44 cm)
Signed lower right 'Nordfeldt'
Titled, estate stamped, and dated on verso on original stretcher bar 'Santa Fe Landscape, 1918-1919'

PROVENANCE
Estate of the artist
Private collection, Santa Fe
By descent in the family
The Owings Gallery, Santa Fe
The Tia Collection, 2014

EXHIBITED
The Owings Gallery, Santa Fe, *Winter Selections* 2015, December 27-March 21, 2015, front and back cover and p.21 (color)

Page 136

ROBERT RAUSCHENBERG (American, 1925-2008)
Renovation
1995
Vegetable dye transfer on paper
60.5 x 96.5 in (153.6 x 245.1 cm)
Signed and dated lower left 'Rauschenberg 95'

PROVENANCE
The artist
Pace Wildenstein, New York
Private collection, Milan
Glenn Dranoff Fine Art, New York
The Tia Collection, 2011

EXHIBITED
Pace Wildenstein, Los Angeles, *Anagrams*, November 15, 1996-January 18, 1997
Pace Wildenstein, New York, *Anagrams*, September 19, 1996-October 19, 1996

ILLUSTRATED
Rauschenberg, Robert. *Anagrams*, New York: Pace Wildenstein, 1996, pl.5 (color)

Page 125

ED RUSCHA (American, born 1937)
Western
1970
Gunpowder and pastel on paper
11.5 x 29 in (29.2 x 73.7 cm)
Signed and dated lower left 'E. Ruscha 1970'

PROVENANCE
The artist
Leo Castelli Gallery, New York
Donald Marron, Mitchell, Hutchins Inc.
Two Trees, New York
Sotheby's, New York, May, 1990, lot 318
James Corcoran Gallery, Santa Monica
Hannah and Russel Kully, San Marino, CA
Edward Tyler Nahem, New York
The Tia Collection, 2013

EXHIBITED
Albright-Knox Art Gallery, Buffalo, *Paintings, Drawings, and Other Works by Edward Ruscha*, June 8-July 11, 1976

ILLUSTRATED
Turvey, Lisa. *Edward Ruscha Catalogue Raisonné of the Works on Paper Volume 1: 1956-1976*, New York: Gagosian Gallery, 2014, p.260 (color)
Ruscha, Ed. *Ed Ruscha: They Called Her Styrene*, London: Phaidon Press Limited, 2000, unpaginated (color)

LISTED
Marshall, Richard D. *Ed Ruscha*, London: Phaidon Press Limited, 2003, p.109
Paintings, Drawings, and Other Works by Edward Ruscha, Albright-Knox Art Gallery, Buffalo, 1976, p.36

Page 143

BILL SCHENCK (American, born 1947)
Gathering Mustangs
2009
Oil on canvas
36 x 36 in (91.44 x 91.44 cm)
Signed and dated lower left 'SCHENCK 09'

PROVENANCE
The artist
The Tia Collection, 2011

Page 14

SEAN SCULLY (American, born Ireland 1945)
Wall of Light Pale Yellow Pink
2009
Oil on aluminum
85 by 75 in (215.9 x 190.5 cm)
Signed on verso

PROVENANCE
The artist (SS995)
Timothy Taylor Gallery, London
The Tia Collection, 2014

EXHIBITED
Timothy Taylor Gallery, London, *Sean Scully: New Work*, May 28-July 3, 2010

Page 101

RICHARD SERRA (American, born 1939)
July #17
2011
Paint stick on handmade paper
46 x 37.1 in (116.8 x 94.3 cm)
SERRA 2011.0031

PROVENANCE
The artist
Gagosian Gallery, Paris
The Tia Collection, 2011

EXHIBITED
Gagosian Gallery, Paris, *Drawings*, November 23, 2011-January 7, 2012

Page 58

JOEL SHAPIRO (American, born 1941)
Untitled
2010
Aluminum (unique)
19.75 x 13 x 23.25 in (50.2 x 33 x 59 cm)
Signed, dated and numbered: 'Shapiro 2010 1896, JS1896'

PROVENANCE
The artist
Galerie Karsten Greve, Paris
The Tia Collection, 2012

EXHIBITED
Galerie Karsten Greve, Cologne, *Joel Shapiro*, September 2-November 6, 2010

Page 48

KETAKI SHETH (Indian, born 1957)
Riddhi and Siddhi, in their living room, Norbury, London, 1997
Gelatin silver print
Edition of 12
Image size: 31 x 30.75 in (78.74 x 78.105 cm)
Paper size: 40 x 35 in (101.6 x 88.9 cm)

PROVENANCE
The artist
The Tia Collection, 2011

EXHIBITED
Fremantle Arts Centre, Perth, Australia, *FotoFreo, The Portrait: Contemporary Indian Photography*, group exhibition, March 17-May 13, 2012
PhotoInk, New Delhi, *Twinspotting*, August 21-October 16, 2010
Art Heritage, New Delhi, *Twinspotting: Photographs of Patel Twins in Britain and India*, 2000

ILLUSTRATED
Sheth, Ketaki and Singh, Raghubir. *Twinspotting: Photographs of Patel Twins in Britain and India*, Manchester, UK: Dewi Lewis Publishing, 1999, cover and p.44

Page 83 and back cover

GIB SINGLETON (American, 1935-2014)
Four Horsemen of the Apocalypse
2001
Bronze
Edition 19 of 25
29 x 33 x 31 in (73.66 x 83.82 x 78.74 cm)
Signed and dated on base 'Singleton 2001'

PROVENANCE
The artist
Galerie Zuger, Santa Fe
The Tia Collection, 2008

Page 35

KIKI SMITH (American, born Germany 1954)
Back Porch Whispering
2012
Cast aluminum with gold leaf (unique)
120 x 48 x 60 in (304.8 x 121.9 x 152.4 cm)

PROVENANCE
The artist
Timothy Taylor Gallery, London
The Tia Collection, 2014

EXHIBITED
Timothy Taylor Gallery, London, *Behold*, October 12-November 17, 2012

Page 65

FRANCIS NEWTON SOUZA (Indian, 1924-2002)
The Virgin of Northampton
1957
Oil on paper mounted to board
48 x 24 in (121.9 x 71.1 cm)
Signed and dated upper left "Souza 57"
Signed, titled, and dated on verso 'F.N. SOUZA ViRGiN of NORTH-AMPTON - 1957'

PROVENANCE
The artist
Harold Kovner, New York
Grosvenor Gallery, London
RDA, London
The Tia Collection, 2010

Page 71

ANTONI TÀPIES (Spanish, 1923-2012)
Esfera i Cadena
1999
Bronze and metal chain
Edition 2 of 6
10.75 x 7.5 x 7.88 in (27.5 x 19 x 20 cm)
Signed and numbered on the bottom

PROVENANCE
The artist
Timothy Taylor Gallery, London
The Tia Collection, 2014

Page 52

CY TWOMBLY (American, 1928-2011)
Untitled (Ramification)
1971
Gouache and wax crayon on paper
32.75 x 27.25 in (83.8 x 69.3 cm)
Signed and dated on verso 'Cy Twombly '71'

PROVENANCE
Galerie Karsten Greve, Paris
The Tia Collection, 2011

Page 144

LAJOS VAJDA (Hungarian, 1908-1941)
Young Laborer
c.1930
Photomontage on cardboard
10 x 8.125 in (25.5 x 20.6 cm)

PROVENANCE
Gallery Erdész, Szentendre, Hungary
The Tia Collection, 2012

EXHIBITED
Royal Museum of Fine Arts, Antwerp, *Lajos Vajda: Touch of Depths*, 2009

Page 94

ANDY WARHOL (American, 1928-1987)
Queen Elizabeth II of the United Kingdom,
from *Reigning Queens*
(Royal Edition)
1985
Screenprint with diamond dust on Lenox Museum Board
Blue background, 1 from the set of 4
39 x 31.5 in (99.06 x 80.01 cm)
Signed lower right 'r ap 4/5 Andy Warhol'
F. & S. II 334-337A

PROVENANCE
Christie's, New York, *Old Master, Modern and Contemporary Prints*, September 15, 2010, lot 210
RDA, London
The Tia Collection, 2010

LISTED
Feldman, Frayda. Schellman, Jörg. *Andy Warhol Prints: A Catalogue Raisonné 1962-1987*, New York: D.A.P. Inc., 2015, p.143

Page 15

CADY WELLS (American, 1904-1954)
New Mexico Landscape
c.1934
Watercolor on paper
15 x 22 in (38.1 x 55.88 cm)
Inscribed lower right 'To Merle'
Signed lower right corner 'Cady Wells'

PROVENANCE
The artist
Gift to Merle Armitage
By descent in his family
Owings-Dewey Fine Art, Santa Fe
Private collection, New Mexico and Hawaii
The Owings Gallery, Santa Fe
The Tia Collection, 2015

Page 20

BERNARD WILLIAMS (American, born 1964)
Bass Reeves-Indian Territory
1999
Oil on canvas
67 x 72.5 in (170.18 x 184.15 cm)
Signed lower right 'BW'

PROVENANCE
The artist
The Tia Collection, 2014

EXHIBITED
Booth Western Art Museum, *A Complex Frontier: Selected Works by Bernard Williams*, May 15-October 5, 2014

Page 145 and front cover

CHRISTOPHER WOOL (American, born 1955)
Untitled
1988
Alkyd on paper
64 x 32 in (163.5 x 81.6 cm)
Signed and dated on verso 'Wool 1988'

PROVENANCE
The artist
Luhring Augustine Gallery, New York
Private collection
Jack Hanley Gallery, San Francisco
Phillips de Pury & Company, New York, Contemporary Art:
Part II, November 13, 2009, lot 248
Serge Maruani, Belgium
The Tia Collection, 2012

EXHIBITED
Patricia Low Contemporary, Geneva, *The Bewildered Image. American Painters from the 1980s*, November 3, 2011-March 10, 2012
Roger Raveel Museum, Machelen-Zulte, Belgium, July, 2010
Luhring Augustine Gallery, New York, 1988

Page 112

Afterword

Modernist Intersections is an exciting exhibition in many ways for The Tia Collection. This is only the second show we have presented with works entirely chosen from the collection. It also represents another collaboration with James Burns, the director of the University of Arizona Museum of Art and a proponent of the collection from our early beginnings.

For the inspired approach to the show themes and title, we are indebted to Olivia Miller, curator at the museum. She synthesized the broad range of artworks that James and I chose from Western to current-day and made the groupings compelling. She has given us the inspiration for a versatile long-term platform from which we can continue to share the collection with audiences around the world.

There is no way one person can keep up with the collector I call "Bob"! In addition to me, he has several other curators, each with distinct areas of knowledge important to the collection: Rob Dean (RDA), whose expertise is the Indian Moderns, French Impressionists, and Indian Mughal miniatures, and Sarah J. McDonald, who is devoted to helping The Tia Collection acquire the best post-war/contemporary works in Europe.

In addition to being an artist whose work is in the collection, Ketaki Sheth is also a friend of the collector. She brought her keen eye as a photographer to highlight subtleties within her medium, while Serena Cattaneo Adorno, who has known Richard Serra for many years, contributed her insight on his work.

I am very grateful to have each of these professionals elucidating the show's ideas and themes. They add a substance of interpretation to the catalogue that I could not have accomplished by myself.

The process of acquiring art includes spending time with the living artists to get to know them beyond their creations, as well as enjoying long-term relationships with many art dealers. We are fortunate to work with the best in their fields and, as a result, privileged to be in the position to consider some of the best works coming to market. Thanks has been given to each dealer by listing their names as part of the provenance for each work in the checklist.

A catalogue like this takes considerable technical expertise to make, and we have the best in their fields helping us to produce something that will last long after the exhibition is over. This is the second time that we have worked together, and I would like to acknowledge Alex Hanna, of Invisible City Designs, the talented graphic designer whose vision and creativity brought all the elements together; our editor, Eve Tolpa, whose ability with words is inspiring and gave all of us an added level of polish; and Jamie Hart, who photographed everything (with the exception of a few works, as noted), giving you the opportunity to experience these pieces just as you would in person.

I hope that this show inspires you to broaden the approach you take when looking at a work of art—considering its maker, the inspiration behind its creation, and how the experience affects your life.

– Laura Finlay Smith, Atelier Art + Advisory

Managing Editor – Laura Finlay Smith
Designer – Alex Hanna / invisiblecitydesigns.com
Copy Editor – Eve Tolpa
Principal Photographpy – James Hart
Color Separations – Fire Dragon Color, Santa Fe, NM
Printer – Prodon, Mumbai, India
Printing Oversight – Rob Dean, RDA
Publisher – The Tia Collection, santafeartadvisor@gmail.com

Note – All dimensions for art work are listed: height x width (x depth).

ISBN – 978-0-9914792-2-1

This catalogue was produced in conjunction with
Modernist Insersections: The Tia Collection
May 14 – October 9, 2016

**U∧ THE UNIVERSITY OF ARIZONA
∧∧ MUSEUM OF ART**